863 Buddhist Ways
to Conquer Life's
Little Challenges

863 Buddhist Ways to Conquer Life's Little Challenges

Barbara Ann Kipfer

Ulysses Press

Published by:
ULYSSES PRESS
P.O. Box 3440
Berkeley, CA 94703
www.ulyssespress.com

ISBN: 978-1-56975-710-9
Library of Congress Control Number 2008911703

Printed in the United States by Bang Printing

10 9 8 7 6 5 4 3 2 1

Managing Editor: Claire Chun
Editor: Richard Harris
Proofreader: Elyce Petker
Production: Judith Metzener, Abby Reser
Cover Design: DiAnna Van Eycke
Interior Design: Lourdes Robles

Distributed by Publishers Group West

Table of Contents

INTRODUCTION

863 Buddhist Ways to Conquer Life's Little Challenges presents a wide array of everyday situations—good, bad, and neutral—faced by many Americans at various stages in their lives and relates them to guidance from the Buddhist teachings. The wisdom, applied to the circumstances found in our ever-changing lives, will help readers make more sense of their existence. The book also provides a solid foundation for the basics of Buddhism. It introduces the precepts, or fundamental ethical rules common to all schools of Buddhism, and applies them to the stuff of daily life. Instead of addressing a handful of questions as in the "What would Buddha do?" books, this volume offers a greater range of situations and addresses them in a succinct and helpful format.

Within the various topics in *863 Buddhist Ways*, the reader will find everyday situations and sayings that offer insight into how to handle those situations. The subject areas and the everyday situations are not just about problems or negativity in life; they also offer Buddhist wisdom in relation to good situations and positive happenings. You can browse through the topics and find situations and wisdom applicable to your own life.

The wisdom offered in this book is based on content from a large number of books about Buddhism, from insight meditation to Zen. The words of those teachers have been adapted to make them more accessible to lay readers. It is all Buddhist wisdom in that the precepts of the Eightfold Path and Four Noble Truths, as well as those found in many of Buddha's other teachings, make up the underlying guidance.

What *863 Buddhist Ways* attempts to do is combine the themes, situations, and sayings of Buddha and the many teachers who have followed after him to give guidance, answers, encouragement, and reinforcement. *863 Buddhist Ways* should serve as a sourcebook for opening the mind and awakening the spirit.

—Barbara Ann Kipfer, Ph.D.

Belief

SITUATION: While you believe in many ideals of Buddhism, you also believe in the power of prayer. From your upbringing and background as a Christian, prayer has always been important in your life. You want that to continue.

WISDOM: *Embrace the adage that "prayer is speaking and meditation is listening."*

SITUATION: Practicing Christianity has been important to you since you were young. You enjoy going to church, and your belief in God is strong. However, you are not afraid to question or disagree with some of the bizarre rituals and beliefs that your religion practices.

WISDOM: *You do not have to give up your Christian, Hindu, Jewish, Islamic, or any other religious beliefs in order to practice a Buddhist-style mindfulness.*

SITUATION: Sometimes it feels as if your prayers go unanswered. Is there any point to praying?

WISDOM: *A good way to pray is to ask that the person you are praying for receive what he or she needs most at this time. You can pray in this way for yourself, too.*

SITUATION: There is one family in your neighborhood that you try to avoid at all costs because they try to push their religious beliefs on you.

WISDOM: *Commit to not harming others through thoughts, words, or deeds. Peace begins with you. Embrace your own spiritual path and you will be fine in such a circumstance because you will bring peace to the situation.*

SITUATION: While you believe in a God who is loving and kind, it is difficult for you to understand how some people think that God would allow people to hurt and kill each other in His/Her name.

WISDOM: *There is always a gap between what a religion says and thinks it is about and what it is actually about. This gap begins with why and how rituals are practiced and how important or unimportant these rituals are.*

SITUATION: You are the first to admit that you do not fully understand the concept of karma. But the idea of karma intrigues you, and you believe it warrants further exploration.

WISDOM: *The law of karma shows you that the way to achieve happiness is by engaging in positive actions and refraining from negative ones. Not only do you yourself create the cause for your future happiness, but, by being kind, ethical, and compassionate toward others, you feel good about yourself while making those around you happy, too.*

SITUATION: Lately, you have been thinking a lot about heaven. It began with a vivid dream you had about your deceased grandfather explaining heaven to you. Since then, heaven has been on your mind.

WISDOM: *There are many unanswered questions about the universe. Does heaven exist? While these questions are interesting, they do not matter on your path of awakening. Spend your time and energy trying to live a peaceful and loving life and gaining wisdom, not pondering questions you can never answer.*

SITUATION: You find it hard to believe that you go to heaven or are reborn into something else. You believe that once you die, that's it.

WISDOM: *The Buddha taught that at the moment of death, the quality of consciousness conditions the arising of a rebirth consciousness. Nothing is carried over, but depending on that last moment, a new consciousness arises.*

SITUATION: When you were in your early teens, you were in a park at dusk with a group of your friends when you all saw what appeared to be a UFO. You all told your parents about the rotating lights on a craft that just hovered over the park for a minute or two and then zoomed away. However, you don't really know if anyone believed you. When the subject of UFOs comes up, you never know if you should say anything about the incident or not.

WISDOM: *All the objects that we perceive in life are created by ourselves. Our perceptions of objects are based on the time and place we are in and will be different from everyone else's.*

SITUATION: Some days you find it hard to believe in anything spiritually, to have faith. When reading the newspaper or watching TV and seeing all the hurt, sadness, and war in the world, it makes you doubt and wonder.

WISDOM: *The remedy for doubt is more understanding. If you are not free from doubt, you will not find freedom. Acceptance and understanding of change is a deep spiritual insight that can transform your life.*

Meditation

SITUATION: In a rush to get to work in the morning, nothing seems to be going right. Even brushing your teeth seems onerous.

WISDOM: *How often in the most mundane tasks have you meditated well?*

SITUATION: You are a beginner to meditation. You don't know if this is normal, but whenever you try to start a meditation, you "hear" constant talking in your head.

WISDOM: *Work toward stopping the internal dialogue, the constant comments of the mind, and break through where the thinking occurs to directly experience the process. When you stop the internal dialogue, you create the ability to wait and to listen.*

SITUATION: You are new at meditation, and it brings many questions. It seems that when you are meditating, you are surrounded by lustful thoughts and feelings. You feel this is getting in the way of your meditation.

WISDOM: *For a week during meditation, be particularly aware each time lust enters your mind state. Watch for it. See what precedes it, how it begins, how long it lasts, and when it ends. Is it a strong or weak mind state? Be aware of mental or physical resistance felt when this mind state arises. Soften and receive. Sit and be aware. Let the mind state arise, observe it, and let it go.*

SITUATION: After dabbling with meditation for a number of years without much success, you are pledging to make a genuine effort in your practice so that you may learn better how to appreciate life in the present moment.

WISDOM: *Five minutes of practice with the sincere desire to wake up to the present moment is worth more than a lifetime of practice without it.*

SITUATION: You are having a personal problem that you do not feel comfortable talking about with anyone. In your mind it is a very private matter that you want to solve on your own terms. You do not want anyone's advice or judgment.

WISDOM: *In many cases, writing about a problem is a good way to solve it. Writing can be a form of meditation. When you write a problem, it helps you experience, feel, and move through it. A simple essay may be the trick for immersing yourself so you can become more mindful and focused on what is bothering you. Grammar, usage, and style are not important. Part of solving your problem is enjoying the process of writing.*

SITUATION: You are going to try to be more honest in everything you do and say. In the past, you used to tell little white lies so you would not hurt other people. But since you began meditation practice, you feel you need to take a next step to progress more.

WISDOM: *Since every aspect of your life is connected to every other aspect of your life, if you tell lies outside of meditation, you cannot expect great truths in meditation.*

SITUATION: Your life is in a perfect storm of emotions. It seems as if you have been in a holding pattern for a long time waiting for things to be resolved. Because of this state, you are easy to anger.

WISDOM: *By learning to hold your mind to an object in meditation, you train in patience. Then, when a moment of anger arises in your everyday life, you may be able to hold your speech and action. Don't jump, lash, or act out. If you are really dedicated to practicing patience, you will even learn to generate love and compassion on the spot when anger arises.*

SITUATION: Your life is extremely hectic. Between work and family, it is difficult keeping everything together and getting through a day without forgetting something. The busier you get, the less organized you become. You waste valuable time running around doing simple things.

WISDOM: *A hectic situation breeds more of the same. To organize your life, begin with your mind. Meditation and deep breathing can help you calm and organize your mind so that you become less distracted and can keep your life in order.*

SITUATION: You made a promise to yourself to find at least 20 minutes every day to meditate. But some days, between family and work responsibilities, it seems impossible to find even 20 minutes you can set aside for meditation.

WISDOM: *Even though life can be overwhelming at times and you can become absorbed by family and work, find some time to simply remember who you really are. Setting aside time to practice your meditation is an important promise you can make to yourself.*

SITUATION: Life has been stressful lately. You seem to be going in a million directions at the same time. You are having trouble sleeping through the whole night. Just as you fall asleep, you wake up in a panic about something that happened during the day. When you wake up in the morning, you are still tired. Your spouse suggests that to combat this cycle, you try meditating before going to bed.

WISDOM: *Use meditation to come mindfully into the moment. Through reflection, appreciate the blessings that fill your life.*

SITUATION: It seems like you are working harder and longer than you used to. Your business is so competitive now that the pressure is intense.

WISDOM: *Meditating while working makes clear the most fundamental precepts. Meditation is not merely a matter of learning to focus and concentrate your mind, but of bringing that state into even the smallest acts of your daily life.*

SITUATION: There does not seem to be enough time in the day to both exercise and meditate on a regular basis. Since you are new to meditation, you are more enthusiastic about meditating than exercising.

WISDOM: *When you begin to practice meditation, do not forget to take care of your body too. Physical health is just as important as spiritual health.*

SITUATION: Saturday morning is your time to be alone and go for a walk at the beach. Everyone in the family knows not to request anything from you during this time.

WISDOM: *Every moment of meditation is a golden opportunity for a fuller, happier life. Feel totally entitled to your meditation period.*

SITUATION: With all that is going on in your life, the last thing you need is troubling dreams at night. But a recurring, disturbing dream keeps waking you up in the middle of the night drenched in fear. You just can't seem to break this nightly pattern.

WISDOM: *To ward off bad dreams, try meditating on an image that you associate with happiness and peace for a few minutes before you go to bed.*

SITUATION: Periodically, it seems that your life goes into a downward spiral and negatively affects everything, including family, friends, and work. It begins with little things going wrong. They add up and become big things going wrong. The spiral is difficult to slow down, let alone stop.

WISDOM: *Feelings are as ephemeral as the weather. The next time you feel yourself going into a downward spiral, turn inward. Instead of distracting yourself with something, sit down and breathe. Meditate and let things be. Meditation allows you to ride out the storms gracefully and detach from your personal ups and downs.*

SITUATION: Getting older is not as much fun as you anticipated. You thought you would feel less confused and more connected with other people. Instead, you are finding yourself confused by just about everything and disconnected from family and friends.

WISDOM: *If you feel confused and disconnected, meditation is the way to straighten out. The heart and the mind gently release. You feel less overwhelmed because you are more centered. You become more effective, more relaxed.*

SITUATION: In retirement, you want to give something back to others. You feel that you have lived a very good life and that it is important to give something back to others.

WISDOM: *You meditate so you can develop your inner potential and actualize your own peak experiences without making them into goals. Mostly, you do it to equip yourself to help other beings.*

SITUATION: You enter a special world when you play the guitar. But when you have a recital or performance in front of other people, you fear that you will forget the music you are supposed to play.

WISDOM: *Meditate on universal love, compassion, awareness, responsibility, energy, peace, calmness, and mindfulness before you play your music. This will help you play in the spirit of your meditation. The music will be just music.*

Animals

SITUATION: You see a spider is crawling on the bedroom ceiling.

WISDOM: *Refrain from killing or harming living beings.*

SITUATION: You try not to kill any living creature when you are outside. In the morning when you get the newspaper and you see worms on your driveway after a rainstorm, you try to gently put them back in the grass. But when an insect or pest enters your house, all bets are off, and you try to eliminate it by any means.

WISDOM: *It feels so much better to gently remove an insect or other pest from inside our home and put it outside than to kill it.*

SITUATION: For your child's birthday, you enroll him in the Save the Manatee Club, making a donation to protect manatees.

WISDOM: *Contemplate the ways humankind exploits animals. Contemplate the many species lost every day. Embrace all animals with your compassion. Wish for your compassion to ease their suffering. Protect life, practice generosity, behave responsibly, and consume mindfully.*

SITUATION: A neighbor's dog bit your child. It was not the first incident this dog was involved in, and the dog had to be destroyed. At a community event, you are seeing the neighbor for the first time since the incident.

WISDOM: *Instead of resisting difficult people and unpleasant situations, allow yourself to open to them and see the suffering underneath. Try looking at them caringly, without reaction. When you open to and feel the suffering of another, compassion has a chance to come forth.*

SITUATION: A barking dog is keeping you from meditating.

WISDOM: *You do not require perfect quiet to meditate. It isn't noise that bothers you, it is your judgment about the noise. Noise is no obstacle to meditation. Accept it. We live in a world of noise.*

SITUATION: A neighborhood dog barks and barks and barks whenever he is left outside by himself. People in the neighborhood have hinted to the neighbor that the dog does this, but she never does anything about it or apologizes. Whenever you hear the dog begin to bark you get very angry.

WISDOM: *It is important to recognize your anger when it first arises and then calm yourself before you react to the situation that caused the anger. Since anger always works against you, it is never a skillful thing to feel.*

SITUATION: Your new job requires a lot from you. Between the traveling, meetings, and report writing, you do not have much left in your tank when you get home. Unfortunately, you do not have the time to play with your dog like you used to or take her for long walks and hikes, and it appears to be having a negative impact on her. She seems to be ignoring you. She no longer runs to the door when you get home or sit on the couch with you when you watch television or read the newspaper.

WISDOM: *Animals want to experience happiness, too. Playing fulfills more than just an evolutionary function. It is also an expression of pleasure and joy. Animals feel pain in their own way, and playing helps them alleviate this suffering and experience freedom.*

SITUATION: Your beloved family dog passed away at a very old age. She led a great life and was a fantastic pet. She was really part of the family. The children want to have a burial for her in the backyard.

WISDOM: *Recognize that everything in life is impermanent. Take solace that within the world of beings, no one has escaped this. Even though you mourn the passing of a beloved pet, be present in this moment and grateful for all you have.*

Nature

SITUATION: You are talking on the telephone to your parents, who have retired from New England to Florida. It is the beginning of fall, and your father mentions that he does miss that first day of the season when you take a deep breath and the air feels different.

WISDOM: *Go outside to take in some deep breaths. Trees and plants are involved in creating the air you breathe. Animals are breathing the same air. So are other humans. Focus on your breathing and look deeply into it. Experience these connections fully.*

SITUATION: You can't remember the last time you felt this good and relaxed. As you hike through the woods on this beautiful fall day, it seems that all your troubles have left you. You want this feeling to remain for a while.

WISDOM: *A rare person sees how far there is to go but remains unhurried, carefully placing each foot on the ground, delighting in the views and sounds without getting lost. The journey is completed in every step.*

SITUATION: As fall comes to an end, you feel slightly depressed thinking about the long winter ahead.

WISDOM: *Live in each season as it passes and resign yourself to the influences of each.*

SITUATION: The winter took a toll on your spirit. Even though spring has sprung, you are having difficulty rejuvenating it.

WISDOM: *Go to a garden and just stand in it. Breathe in the air, the fragrances, the light, the temperature, the music of the plant and animal life. Inhale the energy of these growing things. Recharge your spirit and inner batteries.*

SITUATION: Earth Day is approaching, but you just can't generate much enthusiasm. You feel frustrated because, when you think about it, one person cannot really have a major impact on all the environmental issues the Earth faces.

WISDOM: *Even though the Earth is impermanent, it is our duty to cherish and protect it while we live on it. We may feel frustrated because we cannot solve major environmental problems in a timely fashion. But while we wait for large societal solutions to these problems, we can all take small steps in our own lives to help solve them. Every day should be Earth Day.*

SITUATION: What a day for it to pour down rain. You are in the city waiting for a taxi to take you to an important business meeting. The wetter you get, the madder you get.

WISDOM: *Whatever the day's weather, accept it. To complain about the rain— or lack of it—shows a mind out of tune with nature. Align with nature and accept today's weather. It is needed for life.*

SITUATION: When you were young, you heard your grandparents talking about one of their friends dying. They said the day of his funeral the weather was beautiful. They were sad about that because it is a superstition in their culture that if it rains the day of a person's funeral, they go to heaven. If it does not rain, they don't. While you know this is a silly superstition, every time someone you know passes away, the first thought that comes into your mind is the weather on the day of their funeral.

WISDOM: *Your visions will become clear only when you can look into your own heart. Who looks outside, dreams; who looks inside, awakens.*

SITUATION: Even though you do not have a lot of discretionary funds, you do try to support the local plant-a-tree fundraiser each year in your town. So many trees are cut down in the world, you feel it is important to support organizations that plant them.

WISDOM: *Trees have a positive impact on human health through the emission of natural chemicals. While some of the positive effects are obvious, like removing pollutants from the ground and air and adding CO_2 to the atmosphere, others are not. You also want to show respect for all living things.*

SITUATION: It took successfully protesting the development of a coal-fired power plant in your area for you to wake up and see how important it is to protect nature on a daily basis. During the protest, you met many extremely smart people who have come up with viable alternatives to the coal-fired power plant. For you, this was just the beginning. Now, from the car you drive to the setting of the thermostat in the house, you realize all the little decisions you make concerning the protection of nature are important.

WISDOM: *Protecting nature on a daily basis involves making individual choices rather than just following a set of rules. By basing your actions on generosity, responsibility, wisdom, and respect, you can provide nature the protection she needs in order to flourish.*

SITUATION: You broke the law by demonstrating on the grounds where a coal-fired power plant was going to be built. You and other people violated a court order prohibiting protesters within a certain distance of the building and were arrested.

WISDOM: *Remain mindfully aware of how you use Earth's resources. Cherish the interrelatedness of all life and nourish, rather than deplete, the precious world that is your home. Sometimes you may have to break a little law to call attention to a bigger violation.*

Driving

SITUATION: This is the first spring day that you can drive your convertible with the top down, and it feels good. As you come down the driveway, you realize that you cannot park in the garage because you have too much stuff cluttering it. You know this must change.

WISDOM: *A life cluttered with "things" controls and befuddles you. Ask yourself why you need these items? Could someone else benefit from them? Could your life benefit from being simplified?*

SITUATION: Running a little late for an appointment, you decide to drive faster. You justify your action by telling yourself that you are just keeping up with the traffic.

WISDOM: *Instead, ask yourself, "How important is the appointment? How much time am I actually saving by going too fast?" If you are racing down the road, it's often because your insides are racing rather than feeling calm. Recognize your inherent oneness with the car you are driving and slow down inside, proceeding not in haste but under control.*

SITUATION: Coming to a stop sign, you feel annoyed that it slows your progress.

WISDOM: *The stop sign is a reminder to slow your pace, take a moment's rest, and look around.*

SITUATION: When you drive to work now, not only is your wallet getting lighter, but you are also feeling guilty about the negative impact you are having on the environment. Every time you drive your car to work instead of taking public transportation, your carbon footprint gets bigger.

WISDOM: *Public transportation may not be as convenient as driving a car, but it is time to begin to take responsibility for your actions and respect the limited resources of our Earth. When you truly care about your children—and their children and their children's children—you will break some old habits to create the best possible future for them.*

SITUATION: You see the warning light go on, but you do not want to stop and fill up with gas because you are dressed in your good clothes. You tell yourself your husband can fill up the tank tomorrow. But the next morning on his way to the gas station, he runs out of gas. What should have taken you a few minutes is now costing your husband a lot of extra time.

WISDOM: *Resolve to practice discipline, both mental and physical, that will lead to greater freedom, skill, and joy in your everyday life.*

SITUATION: While driving to work one morning, you see a squirrel on the side of the road deciding whether to cross or not. You're in a rush for work, so you do not slow down. Unfortunately, the squirrel makes the wrong decision, runs into the road in front of your car, and gets hit. In your mind it was an accident, but you wonder if you should have at least slowed down a bit when you saw the squirrel.

WISDOM: *It is wise to have compassion for animals because you may have been one in another lifetime.*

SITUATION: One of the more frustrating events in life is being stuck in traffic on the highway and seeing cars zoom by you, cutting in front of you to get a better position. It feels like that they think their lives are more important than yours.

WISDOM: *By following a few simple rules when you are stuck in highway traffic, you can turn the experience into an opportunity for personal growth. There is an art to dealing with traffic jams. Remain calm. Take three deep, conscious, cleansing breaths. Think of all the other drivers' needs. Visualize the traffic system running smoothly. Remain in your lane and leave enough room in front of you so you can invite all cars in while driving at a steady speed, trying not to use the brakes, in order to create a zipper merging that keeps the traffic flowing.*

SITUATION: Returning home from work, you experience your first road rage incident. A car comes flying up behind you and the driver starts honking the horn, flashing their lights, and waving his arms. You're going the speed limit, so you maintain your current course. After about a mile, you become a little frightened and get off the road so the car can pass. As it does, the driver makes an inappropriate gesture toward you.

WISDOM: *Mindful driving protects us and others. If angry drivers want to pass you in haste, let them. They are not driving mindfully. Where they're going is not the way. Driving mindfully lies in saying, "After you."*

SITUATION: You are speeding to get home from work so you can attend your son's school event when a police officer pulls you over. As he approaches your car, you are trying to come up with a response to the obvious question he is going to ask: "Do you know that you were speeding?"

WISDOM: *When you acknowledge your intentions and take responsibility for them, you have the genuine possibility of transforming yourself. You may want to say things or offer up excuses to help your cause, but do not say them if they are dishonest.*

SITUATION: Unfortunately, on your way home from work, you witness a horrible traffic accident where someone lost their life. You are so shaken by the event that you cannot stop thinking about how the person in the accident was here one second and gone the next.

WISDOM: *Death is certain, but time of death is uncertain. We just do not know how much time we have left to fulfill our potential. Ask yourself every day, "How can I make the best use of this day?"*

SITUATION: Although you love your big SUV and feel safe in it, you are beginning to feel guilty about the poor gas mileage it gets and the carbon footprint you are leaving. When you fill up with gas, your children say, "There goes my college money."

WISDOM: *Rely on your wisdom to bring your actions into harmony with your deepest values. Wisdom will help you purify your actions to cultivate what is right and abandon what is wrong.*

SITUATION: Growing up in the South, you're not used to driving in the snow. On your way home from work, you get caught in a big snowstorm. You just want to get home safely.

WISDOM: *Practice mindful breathing when driving in difficult conditions or heavy traffic. Breathing consciously will bring more awareness and concentration and help you avoid accidents.*

SITUATION: You witness a hit-and-run accident. You see and write down the license plate of the car that hit the other car and caused injury. You report the crime and give the police the information. You are a little dismayed that no one contacts you to say thank you.

WISDOM: *If you help others and expect a pat on the back, then it is not selfless service. But if you help others and do not expect a pat on the back, then you learn the lesson of selfless service and realize that you benefit as much as the people you are helping.*

SITUATION: On the highway, your car gets a flat tire and you have to pull over to the breakdown lane. You are frightened to get out of your car because other vehicles are going so fast. A stranger pulls up behind your car to offer help. After the tire is changed and you're on your way again, you realize how lucky you were to have someone help you.

WISDOM: *Appreciate each moment as a vehicle for developing wisdom.*

SITUATION: On a family vacation in the mountains, your car goes off the road and crashes into a tree. No one in the car is seriously hurt, but you all have minor injuries. The area is very desolate, and you have no cell phone service. It is getting late, and you are getting scared about your situation.

WISDOM: *Do not doubt your abilities or give up hope. Show your resolve to take action and do the best you can under the difficult circumstances. It is better to take some type of action than to do nothing.*

SITUATION: You have a lead foot. To keep up with your busy life and schedule, you tend to drive a bit above the speed limit. It seems like you are always a little late for a meeting or appointment, so you try to make up the time in the car. Unfortunately, one time when you are speeding, you get into a car accident. While there are no serious injuries, you get a ticket for speeding and causing the accident.

WISDOM: *To be a safe driver, you must be in control of your car as well as your mind. Cars are dangerous weapons, especially when you don't follow the rules. When you have control of your mind, driving the speed limit is a natural thing to do. You do not feel anger, frustration, or rage at what is happening around you on the road. You become a safer driver. And if you have control at the wheel, most likely you will have control in other areas of your life as well.*

SITUATION: You are taking your grandmother to the doctor to help your parents out while they are on vacation. When your grandmother opens the car door, she hits another parked car with the door. You don't want to embarrass her, so you pretend not to see what happened. You are not sure if any damage was done to the other car or if your grandmother even realized that she hit it .

WISDOM: *Be sorry for deeds that you should worry about, not those you need not worry about.*

SITUATION: You are in the passenger seat in a car accident, and your friend is the driver. Neither of you is hurt, but the car is damaged pretty badly. Your friend, who owns the car, is pretending to be injured so he can file a fraudulent claim with the other driver's insurance company for a considerable sum of money. He has asked you to go along with his plan to help him out.

WISDOM: *You should always tell the truth. Even if you think a lie will help someone or you think it is a small lie, you should still tell the truth. Lying contradicts reality, so it will never help. It may appear to help in the short run, but in the long run lying is never helpful.*

SITUATION: No one, including you, seems to be following the new law that prohibits talking on the cell phone while driving. When you get an incoming phone call, you do answer it.

WISDOM: *Mindfully embrace the freedom to make choices—part of what living in the moment affords you.*

SITUATION: You have a strict rule for your 17-year-old driver: no talking on the cell phone while driving. On your way home from work, you see him driving and talking on the cell phone.

WISDOM: *Discuss it calmly and forgive the incident. Mindfully acknowledge that others, like yourself, are still growing. Forgive this, just as you often have to forgive yourself for offenses. Safety is the issue, so give the blessing of a loving heart while teaching this lesson.*

SITUATION: When you are alone in the car, you become a rock star. You know that you don't have a good voice, but you enjoy singing your favorite songs. When other cars approach beside you, you become a ventriloquist and sing with your lips closed. You would be embarrassed if anyone heard or saw you singing.

WISDOM: *Let the immediacy of music touch your deepest feelings and open your heart and mind to all of your senses. Music touches and resonates with the senses. Cultivate this and interact with all of the world the way you do with music.*

SITUATION: It is your natural tendency to speed up when you see a yellow light. Now that you are teaching your teenager to drive, you're not sure what to tell him to do when he comes to a yellow light.

WISDOM: *Try to change your approach. By saying "after you" and stopping at a yellow light, you begin to calm the mind and eliminate the rushing. You start to flow with the traffic, not fight it.*

SITUATION: Your 17-year-old daughter gets a traffic ticket for speeding. She has only had her driver's license for six months, and the speeding ticket was for going 45 mph in a 30 mph zone.

WISDOM: *Teach her to stay awake, slow down, and notice. It will help in so many ways. Mindful awareness slows things down.*

SITUATION: When you were 18 years old, you got arrested for driving under the influence of alcohol. You are not proud of the incident, but you learned a valuable lesson and have never driven a car again after having even one drink. Now, nine years later, you are applying for graduate school and the school wants you to write an essay on what you learned from the incident.

WISDOM: *Because of our inherent Buddha nature, our positive qualities are stronger and more numerous than our negativities. But because of habitual mind, we focus on our ignorance. Admitting ignorance about that incident need not be negative. Focus on the positive results. Wisdom cuts through ignorance and leads to true freedom.*

SITUATION: Your teenager is turning 16 years old soon, and you and your spouse are discussing the car options that are available. Do you let her have her own car, or do you let her borrow one of yours? While it would be nice to gain the time back that you spend transporting her around to practices and school activities, you are concerned about whether she is ready for the awesome responsibility of a car.

WISDOM: *Your faith determines your destiny. Have faith in the metamorphosis that is about to take place. Let your child become a butterfly and touch the flowers. Sometimes you have to make decisions or take actions on faith and open to the great unknown. Use the power of faith to dispel doubt and open to life's mysteries and joys.*

SITUATION: During the holiday season, you usually make the long drive to your parents' house with someone else. This year you will be making the trip alone. Traveling by yourself feels a little weird.

WISDOM: *When traveling alone, enjoy your seclusion without desire. Tranquility is fostered by solitary time.*

SITUATION: You're trading in your old car for a new one. The dealer asks you if the car was ever involved in an accident. You were in a minor fender-bender that you got repaired. You will get a lower price on the trade-in if the dealer knows the car was in an accident.

WISDOM: *The Buddha knew that thinking, speaking, and acting in ethical ways were preliminary steps to take before progressing to higher spiritual development.*

SITUATION: Waiting your turn at the Department of Motor Vehicles, you just don't understand why the line always has to be long. Can't they ever get their act together and become more efficient? It seems like a huge waste of your time.

WISDOM: *A simple, mindful exercise that you can do when you are waiting in a long line is to take a break from your usual thoughts and complaints and wake up and look at the magical and vast world around you.*

SITUATION: When you go to the Department of Motor Vehicles to get your driver's license renewed, you are asked whether you want to become an organ donor. Without even thinking, you fill out the form to participate in the program. What are the spiritual implications of your decision?

WISDOM: *Is karma involved in organ donation? Your karma, like fruit, ripens from thoughts and actions you have planted. You do not know when it will manifest, but each thought and action will manifest someday. Be mindful of what you do in the moment to sow karmic seeds of happiness for yourself and the world.*

Travel

SITUATION: The train is really crowded for today's commute, and the air conditioning just stopped working.

WISDOM: *In your mind, see a mountain lake with a smooth, glasslike surface. A breeze sends ripples across the water. As the breeze subsides, the ripples do too, and the water is smooth again. Remember this during the day, whenever something ruffles or disturbs you. Recall the image of the mountain lake, feel the ripples, and then let them settle.*

SITUATION: You are feeling yourself growing agitated as an announcement is made over the loud speaker that your plane is delayed because of mechanical problems.

WISDOM: *Patience means taking a few deep breaths instead of yelling in frustration.*

SITUATION: The captain of the airplane just announced that the flight has been diverted to another airport because of poor weather conditions.

WISDOM: *Patience has three essential aspects: gentle forbearance, calm endurance of hardship, and acceptance of the truth.*

SITUATION: You feel responsible for picking the family vacation destination. You have always wanted to go to Hawaii, and the rest of the family agreed to it. Unfortunately, the weather has not cooperated. It has rained almost every day you've been here.

WISDOM: *Don't think you are carrying the whole world on your shoulders. Make it fun, make it easy, make it play. It is more productive and a lot more enjoyable to respond creatively than to react cantankerously. So relax and enjoy the ride.*

SITUATION: On vacation, the weather is terrible, the hotel room is too small, the children are not behaving well, and the whole trip is very expensive. You feel like the vacation is a failure.

WISDOM: *Do not fixate on stress or trauma—just let go. If you don't attach to the things that cause you stress, they can't cause you stress.*

SITUATION: You are terrified of flying, especially over water, because you think the plane will crash and you will end up stranded on an deserted island. But, your spouse really wants to take a special anniversary vacation to Hawaii, and you do not want to deny her.

WISDOM: *Remain calm and reasonable. Be aware that you want happiness, you want to be rid of suffering, and you have the right to accomplish these goals. Consider that we often work long and hard and are willing to make temporary sacrifices for a long-term goal. One person can make sacrifices in order to help a larger good. The point is that you must serve and help other beings.*

SITUATION: While taking a vacation in New York City, you get lost and end up in a part of town that does not look too friendly or safe. It is beginning to get dark, and you are becoming anxious about finding your way back to your hotel.

WISDOM: *Fear is a sign of opportunity. Refrain from the actions that create more fear and confusion.*

Food and Drink

SITUATION: Your whole life you have eaten three meals a day at about the same times each day. Food has become a habit, a kind of ritual. You are trying to become more spiritual in your approach to eating food.

WISDOM: *The horse in the field knows nothing of breakfast, lunch, and dinner. It eats when hungry. Follow that same kind of naturalness.*

SITUATION: You are pouring that first cup of tea or coffee or glass of milk in the morning.

WISDOM: *Train yourself to drink your tea, coffee, or milk mindfully.*

SITUATION: Growing up in a house of coffee drinkers, drinking coffee was a very natural and acceptable thing to do. But now you are trying to get pregnant, and you feel you should cut out caffeine.

WISDOM: *The next time you drink coffee, instead of spacing out or doing it automatically, turn it into a meditation. Pay close attention as you sip. Notice how your body feels. Whenever your mind drifts off, bring it back to the experience. Do this with full awareness. Do this the next time and the next time and see if your awareness grows.*

SITUATION: It seems you have many things going on at one time. You are just so busy. You feel you are a good multitasker, but in the morning when you eat your breakfast and read the newspaper, you feel that you are not getting any satisfaction from these activities.

WISDOM: *When you eat and read the newspaper, just eat and read the newspaper. Be aware of the doing.*

SITUATION: At lunchtime, you switch to automatic pilot. You wait in the same line and eat the same foods every day in your workplace cafeteria. You nod to the same people and sit at the same table. It seems as if you are looking at yourself in black-and-white instead of color.

WISDOM: *Find a way to punctuate your life with mindful moments so you create little gaps that take your mind off automatic pilot. Whether through deep breathing, meditation, pausing, or listening, wake up and see the amazing world that surrounds you and connect with the greatness of life. Don't let this magic escape you.*

SITUATION: It seems that life is very busy now. There is just not much free time between work, family, activities, and responsibilities. The first thing that gets neglected is dinner. There is just no time to cook—or even eat— a healthy meal.

WISDOM: *Meals can be a wonderful time to sit down, relax, and connect with your family. They can be a great opportunity for conversation. Eating and food can be woven into the fabric of your life.*

SITUATION: Every meal your son eats at the kitchen table is a messy affair. No matter how many times over the years you tell him, nicely and sternly, the mess still occurs.

WISDOM: *Instead of being angry over nuisances, irritations, and frustrations, accept such instances with either humor, calm serenity, or constructive efforts to improve the situation. It may be as simple as realizing that this problem will be meaningless as time passes.*

SITUATION: Every Friday night has been pizza night for as long as you can remember. You are content with this routine, but other family members want to change it and add a little variety to life.

WISDOM: *Freedom and happiness are found in flexibility and the ease with which you deal with change. Be like water flowing—never fighting, flexible, yet persistent.*

SITUATION: Your children are fussy eaters. They love one particular tomato sauce you have been using for years, but the last time you went to the store to buy some, it was no longer on the shelf. Upon further investigation, you discover that the sauce is no longer being made.

WISDOM: *Attachment/aversion polarity is the source of all our suffering. Our attitude toward what we encounter in life creates suffering. Attachment and aversion put us at war with life's basic reality: things change. What we want and what we don't want come to us and then go away.*

SITUATION: It is extremely difficult to get your children to try new foods, especially healthy ones. Every time you attempt to introduce them to new and healthy foods, a battle ensues. It seems the harder you try, the more limited their choices become.

WISDOM: *Changing the eating habits of children is challenging but not impossible. Lure them with the beauty of nature and how food is grown. Get them involved in the growing, picking, and preparation of wholesome foods. They will begin to learn the interconnectedness between themselves and food. When they eat something delicious and healthy that they had a part in creating, they develop a more positive relationship with food.*

SITUATION: It is difficult to please everyone in your family in terms of what to cook for dinner. You want to plan healthy meals, but you also don't want every meal to be an argument about the food.

WISDOM: *Eating choices produce a measurable cause and effect on our bodies. The food we eat changes the way we look and feel. It can even change our moods.*

SITUATION: What could be better? It is a beautiful day outside and you are preparing a salad with locally grown ingredients that look beautiful.

WISDOM: *Happy cooks make happy food.*

SITUATION: Time is short, and you are feeling pressure to create the perfect holiday meal for your entire family.

WISDOM: *Remind yourself to pause and reflect on food's higher purpose at every meal. Let go of any wish for the food or the meal or the occasion to be "perfect."*

SITUATION: One of your relatives never invites you over to their house. It seems that all the holidays are celebrated at your house. It is expensive and time-consuming to put on these affairs. Then, at last, the relative finally invites you to her house for a lunch.

WISDOM: *Be grateful for the meal, no matter how simple. Stay in the present moment and let go of thoughts of the past and future.*

SITUATION: Baking special holiday cookies began with your grandmother and mother. You have taken over the tradition with your children and grandchildren. Giving the cookies is enjoyable, but baking them is the most enjoyable part.

WISDOM: *Do not believe in or do something solely because someone has told you so or because of tradition or because many others do. Test for yourself, experience for yourself. Your own experience brings understanding and, often, joy.*

SITUATION: There is no one home. Ice cream is in the freezer. You really feel like eating it.

WISDOM: *Guilt is a feeling many of us attach to food. You may feel guilty about eating too much or not enough or of eating the "wrong" thing. These feelings are just as damaging as the foods. Whatever you eat, eat it with full awareness and joy for every bite.*

SITUATION: Every time you have a particularly difficult day at work, you automatically go for the carton of ice cream when you get home. You just don't know why you continue to do this. The ice cream does not even taste good any more, and it only makes you feel relieved for a few moments.

WISDOM: *Mindfulness gives you the time you need to prevent and overcome negative patterns of thought and behavior. Mindfulness helps you cultivate and maintain positive patterns. It gets you to turn off the automatic pilot and helps you take charge of your thoughts, words, and deeds.*

SITUATION: The kids are having their dessert. You've had a tough work day and have a craving for some dessert, too. How about nice cold ice cream on a hot summer evening?

WISDOM: *If you choose to have dessert, enjoy every bite without guilt. Appreciate the effort of all hands, both seen and unseen, that labored to create this dessert.*

SITUATION: You realize that it is wise to cut down on eating meat for health and environmental reasons, but you sure love a good steak.

WISDOM: *Be aware of the food you are eating. A vegetarian diet uses approximately fifteen times less water than a meat-based diet.*

SITUATION: When you look in the mirror, you notice that you have gained a bit of weight. You can't stop thinking about food. It seems as if you are always hungry.

WISDOM: *A way to deal with recurring obsessive thoughts is to call them tapes or reruns. Every time they pop into your head, say "Tape!" or "Rerun!" Noting desires with humor can help get your mind out of its rut.*

SITUATION: You are thinking of radically changing your diet because of the benefit to both you and the environment.

WISDOM: *The foods that are healthiest for the human body are also the healthiest for our environment and create the least suffering for other creatures.*

SITUATION: Growing up in the Midwest, eating and enjoying steak was a very natural thing to do. But in recent years, because of the social issues regarding meat, you have cut down on the amount of meat that you eat and would like to eliminate it from your diet. It is very hard to do. When you don't eat meat for a week, the hamburger at the next table sure looks good.

WISDOM: *While it is difficult to give up meat, vegetarianism is a natural extension of Buddhism. Besides the spiritual cost of slaughtering animals to put meat on our tables, there is also a huge environmental and social cost. Global warming, food shortages, and higher food costs are all attributed to putting meat on our plates.*

SITUATION: Busy, busy, busy. There just does not seem to be enough time. You have the kids in the car, and you are stopping at a fast-food restaurant for dinner.

WISDOM: *You can eat mindfully anywhere—even at a fast-food restaurant.*

SITUATION: You're dining at one of your favorite local restaurants. The waitress for your table is one of your neighbor's children whom you have known for a long time. You hate to say it, but the service she provided was poor.

WISDOM: *Mindfully examine your opinions with an open heart and clear mind. Your attachment to your opinions is a key source of suffering, especially with family and friends. Let go of your opinions and rigid conceptions.*

SITUATION: Your spouse wants to go to a new ethnic restaurant in town. You did not even know this country had a food specialty. Your spouse will try any type of food that is put in front of him, but you are not an adventurous eater, so this is going to be a big challenge for you.

WISDOM: *Be mindful when eating. Be present with your willingness to try this new cuisine. Be thankful for the gift of food in your life. At each meal, wish that all beings everywhere may have enough to eat.*

SITUATION: You have been in the mood for Italian food all day. When you get home from work, you ask your wife if she would like to go out to eat dinner. She says yes but then adds that she has been in the mood for Chinese food all day long.

WISDOM: *Compromise is the cornerstone of relationships. Each time you are in such a situation, one of you will have a stronger motivation to make the other happy. Is it you today? Instead of grasping onto what you what, acknowledge that the other person also wants happiness. Cultivate openheartedness and appreciate the blessings of your life. Tonight, how about General Tso's?*

SITUATION: The meal at the nice restaurant is pretty expensive. While the food is excellent, you are becoming full—but you continue to eat because you paid for it.

WISDOM: *Use right understanding when you feel obsessed with food, when you're jealous of someone who does not have a problem with food, when you feel anxious about overeating at a restaurant or party, or when you "love" a certain kind of food. Become mindful of your relationship to food and more aware of your automatic behaviors around eating.*

SITUATION: The steak you ordered at an expensive, highly rated restaurant was not cooked enough for your liking. When the waiter came back with the steak after you requested that it be cooked more, it went from undercooked to overcooked. You felt bad that you had to complain about it again.

WISDOM: *Genuine happiness is living in a simple, direct way, without cluttering up the mind by wanting things, hating things, judging, taking too much, worrying, or doubting. In a situation like this, do what you can or must, but then let go. It is just one meal.*

SITUATION: Happy hour is in full swing. Your friends are urging you to have another drink. Although that sure sounds good, you are driving after the party, and you have had your one drink, the limit you put on yourself.

WISDOM: *Observe your impulses to use intoxicants and become aware of what is going on in your heart and mind at the time of those impulses.*

SITUATION: At school there is a lot of peer pressure to drink alcohol. Everyone talks about partying and drinking. You have no desire to drink alcohol because it is illegal at your age and you feel that it will get in the way of your training and schooling. But you also don't want to feel alienated because you limit your friendships to only people who don't party and drink.

WISDOM: *Do not follow the crowd, but don't complain about those who do.*

SITUATION: At a college party, you overdo it, drink too much alcohol, and get sick. When the party was starting, it seemed like all the other people were having a great time drinking. Lying in bed, you realize that you did not know when enough was enough.

WISDOM: *There is no point in trying to learn from those who have nothing to teach. Unmindful consumption causes suffering.*

SITUATION: After you graduate from college and find a job, drinking alcohol is just not doing what it did for you earlier. However, your friends still like to party like they did in college.

WISDOM: *If you drink, know your limit. If you abstain, do not judge those who partake. The path to the truth lies in the middle way between opposites.*

SITUATION: When you have a tough day at work, you automatically think about going to happy hour or drinking at home.

WISDOM: *In moments of emotional confusion, the pathway of wise avoidance can be your lifeline to simplicity and calm. Wise avoidance may involve taking your attention out of the familiar groove of your habits. You need to see a habit as a habit—something you do not need to be bound to.*

SITUATION: Growing up, alcohol was always around your house and freely consumed. It was not until you got older that you realized your parents had a drinking problem. Now that they are older, you are seeing the physical effects of this habit on them. You love your parents and are concerned for their health.

WISDOM: *By helping parents identify an addiction with compassion and without judgment, you offer them the ability to find strength in themselves so they can liberate themselves from the addiction.*

SITUATION: At a spaghetti dinner fundraiser you are helping to host at your child's school, one of the elderly customers complains about the amount of food they got and the cost of the event.

WISDOM: *Approach difficult situations with enthusiasm. The mind will be energized and better able to meet the challenge. This approach is more useful than the pessimistic one.*

SITUATION: Food is a crutch for you. When you feel pressure and unhappiness, food changes your mood. When you are relaxed and happy, you use food to celebrate. After a big meal, even if you are full, you still eat dessert. You deserve it.

WISDOM: *While eating, honor the conservation of resources before and during your meal. Make sure the portion on your plate is not too large. Eat everything on your plate. Become aware of your food and appreciate what it is for.*

SITUATION: The scale keeps going up, and the clothes keep getting tighter. You know that you should watch your weight, but eating what you like is a pleasurable and satisfying experience. In fact, these days, it seems like one of the few pleasures left that you thoroughly enjoy.

WISDOM: *Eating healthy and nutritious food does not have to detract from the joy of eating. Using food as medicine can improve your health and still be pleasurable and satisfying.*

SITUATION: You are trying to get in better physical shape and eat healthier foods. Over the years, you have let your body and diet go a bit. This seems like a good time to begin getting in better shape and eating healthier. You are trying to persuade your spouse to join you in exercising more and eating healthier foods.

WISDOM: *Trying to persuade someone else to change is never wise. It is just an excuse. Changing yourself is the best way to help ourselves and at the same time set an example for others.*

SITUATION: Over the years, during stressful times in your life, you have developed an eating disorder. It is very easy for you to get caught up in either eating too little or too much, depending on how you feel your life is going.

WISDOM: *Learn to recognize when you are using food in a way that is mindless, defensive, or protective. Keep coming back to the present moment—the Zen of eating. Have your feelings and then release them. Stuffing yourself to dull feelings of loneliness or fear impacts you negatively. You are interfering with your wholeness and personal growth.*

SITUATION: One of your daughter's friends confided in her that she is suffering from anorexia. You overheard the conversation by accident. You do not want to come across as a busybody, but you also do not want the girl to suffer.

WISDOM: *Certain behaviors can either lead to nourishment or suffering. Compassion is based on knowing that all human beings have an innate desire to be happy and overcome suffering, just like you.*

SITUATION: By the amount of weight she has lost, it has become obvious that your daughter has an eating disorder. While she is at college, it is very difficult for you to address the situation, but you want to get involved because you love her so much.

WISDOM: *There is a distinction between realizing that a person needs to make some lifestyle changes to experience better health and having that person actually change. The work is in finding ways to talk to them so that they make positive changes in their habits.*

SITUATION: To help end world hunger, you have joined a local farm co-op that distributes excess food to homeless shelters. Even though the farm is on only an acre of land, you feel good about what it does.

WISDOM: *Hunger, like all suffering in this world, is caused by greed, hatred, and delusion. Alleviate suffering wherever you see it by whatever means are available to you. A great way to influence others is by setting a good example yourself.*

SITUATION: You do not enjoy food like you used to. Now, it just seems that you eat to stay alive. There is no longer enjoyment in preparing and eating meals.

WISDOM: *Be grateful and do not take for granted that you are able to fill your bowl when so many in this world cannot. Next time you eat a meal, show appreciation to those who work out of sight to plant, raise, harvest, and prepare the food for your comfort. Remember them and be grateful for them.*

SITUATION: Every afternoon at work, you get one of those high-calorie specialty coffee drinks. The afternoon jolt is nice, but your wallet is becoming smaller, and your stomach is becoming bigger because of these drinks.

WISDOM: *When you get pleasure and a sense of happiness from just inhaling the smell of food, you can cut your expenses and lower your caloric intake. Instead of ordering the specialty coffee, just walk by the coffee shop, take a deep breath, and enjoy that.*

SITUATION: It is a little bit more expensive and a little bit of a hassle to get, but you are beginning to understand the importance of purchasing and eating locally grown organic food. You are even thinking of joining a local co-op farm that grows organic food.

WISDOM: *Food safety, both for humans and the Earth, is a real-world problem. One solution is to grow and eat locally grown organic food. By reframing the problem in a solvable way, we can help save the Earth. We can be the ones who change the world and overcome the obstacles to a sustainable future.*

SITUATION: While you will be the first to admit that you are not the best chef in the world, you did work hard to make a special meal for your boyfriend. The experiment was time-consuming and costly and did not turn out well at all. Your boyfriend was gracious about it, but you still feel really bad.

WISDOM: *The key to cooking good food is to use fresh and locally grown ingredients—organic if possible. It does not have to be complicated or expensive to be good. The way fruits and vegetables are grown affects their flavor. Like with other matters, the right seeds need to be planted in the right place and cared for in the right way and they need to be picked at the right moment and eaten quickly.*

SITUATION: You grew up in the Midwest with no strong ethnic background, but you married into an ethnic family that prides themselves on their cooking. No matter how hard you try, you cannot replicate the meals that your relatives prepare. While you know everyone appreciates the effort and work you put into preparing meals, you can tell that the outcome does not meet the standards they are used to and your feelings get hurt.

WISDOM: *That we take ourselves so seriously, that we are so absurdly important in our own minds, is a problem for us. Zen reminds us of how pointless it is to take ourselves too seriously. Life is too short.*

SITUATION: Every year you give up a food or drink item for Lent. Some years you are successful at giving the item up, other years you are not. You often wonder if this sacrifice makes any difference in your life. What is the purpose?

WISDOM: *No one really knows for sure if the rituals we perform are good or bad for us. But even if you are confused about the practice or doubt its worth, if something does work in your life, like sacrificing during Lent, then keep on doing it. This sacrifice probably makes you a better person, so why discontinue it?*

SITUATION: While shopping for milk, you notice that the expiration date on the carton had already passed. You place it back on the shelf without telling a store employee.

WISDOM: *Be aware of your laziness and procrastination. Bring timely energy to do what needs to be done.*

SITUATION: You are hosting a neighborhood party at your house. During the hors d'oeuvres, you see one of the neighbors double-dipping his chips in the salsa. You notice that a couple of other people see the same thing. You don't know if you should say something to the double-dipping guest.

WISDOM: *You have witnessed something that may be harmful to others' health. At some time or other, we all act in ways that harm others. When someone commits a harmful act, see if you can create conditions for happiness and break the cycle. Through mindfulness, compassion, and kindness, help generate conditions of happiness for those who cause harm to other beings.*

Home

SITUATION: When you are washing the dishes, you feel like you are on autopilot or in another place.

WISDOM: *Really do what you are doing. Be awake and alive as you do it, mindful of the tendency to go on autopilot.*

SITUATION: Turning on a light, you often don't think about the process that makes it possible.

WISDOM: *The understanding of how things happen becomes the gateway to the very highest kind of happiness.*

SITUATION: It seems like no one appreciates your effort and all the time you spend doing laundry. Today is one of those days, and it's getting to you. You are trying to fight that feeling.

WISDOM: *The time you spend doing everyday tasks is precious. It is a time for being alive. When you practice mindful living, peace will bloom during your daily activities.*

SITUATION: Busy houses can become overwhelming at times. You find that it is easy to lose your mindfulness.

WISDOM: *Many things happen every day that you can use as bells of mindfulness: the doorbell, telephone, turning on a light, flushing a toilet.*

SITUATION: The next time you light a candle to enhance the atmosphere, reflect on the symbolism of the candle.

WISDOM: *Thousands of candles can be lit from a single candle, and the life of the candle will not be shortened. Happiness never decreases by being shared.*

SITUATION: To save more college money, you and your family have decided to begin cleaning the house yourselves. Each family member has a specific task. You want to make this project a life lesson.

WISDOM: *The clean house isn't the goal. The process of cleaning is the goal.*

SITUATION: Laundry day has become an everyday chore. You can't imagine how your family can create so many dirty clothes. What once was not a bad job has become a big pain because it seems like you spend a tremendous amount of time doing laundry.

WISDOM: *A project or chore that you don't want to do is exactly what you make it: something interesting or a pain. Your pick. Challenge yourself to think about a dreaded chore as a possibility for happiness.*

SITUATION: When someone at work gives you some tomatoes from their garden at home, you cannot help but notice the smile and sense of accomplishment on their face. It so inspires you that you decide to start your own garden.

WISDOM: *Gardening releases physical tension and reduces the amount of stress hormones circulating in the body, while the act of cultivation in itself is soothing for the soul.*

SITUATION: Work was unbelievable today because of the big snowstorm. What could have gone wrong went wrong today. As you get close to your house, you remember that the driveway needs to be shoveled.

WISDOM: *When clearing the snow, try focusing all of your attention on your hands. Note the sensations. If a thought comes, let it go and refocus on your hands.*

SITUATION: Chaos has broken out. You've brought work home from the office. Two kids need to get to practice. And to top it off, dinner has to somehow appear.

WISDOM: *The combination of effort, inner detachment, and genuine equanimity helps you come home within yourself and find inner peace.*

SITUATION: Every neighborhood has one house all the kids gravitate to. It is exhausting when that is your house.

WISDOM: *Be happy where you are. Learn that locked within the moments of each day are all the joys and peace you want. Be the place where the good times are.*

SITUATION: Between running to someone's game, fixing up the yard, and all the other things that need to be accomplished, the weekends seem so busy that it is difficult to feel like you are enjoying them.

WISDOM: *The essence of mindfulness in daily life is to make every moment you have your own. Even if you are hurrying, hurry mindfully. If you find your mind compelling you to get every last thing done—remind yourself that some of it can probably wait. Or stop completely and ask, "Is this worth it?"*

SITUATION: Every time you notice that something in the house has moved slightly, you feel that you must put it in its proper place. Unfortunately, a family member usually makes a hurtful comment when your compulsive behavior kicks in.

WISDOM: *You do not need to indulge the mind's every desire and impulse. Learn to say no to the mind, gently and with humor. Even if someone says something to hurt you, learn to say nothing unless it is positive or helpful.*

SITUATION: Getting a new car or remodeling the kitchen just does not fill you up with happiness anymore.

WISDOM: *Genuine happiness and peace lie in contentment and simplicity. We don't need very much to be happy.*

SITUATION: In your house, the TV is always on, whether anyone is watching it or not. You find yourself stopping whatever you are doing to watch the TV, even though you didn't plan to.

WISDOM: *The precept about intoxicants is to not partake of them or to at least avoid them. This includes excessive TV watching, computer use, and unhealthy eating. These activities cloud and confuse the mind.*

SITUATION: Your roommate is constantly reminding you to keep your room and the rest of the apartment clean. She keeps her area very clean.

WISDOM: *Clean up your room. The way of Zen is to clean as you go.*

SITUATION: Your children have been studying the effects of consumption and recycling at school. Now they are getting on your case about recycling.

WISDOM: *By learning to recognize what to consume and what to reuse, you keep your mind and body healthy and preserve the Earth.*

SITUATION: You hate to go on vacation, even for one night, because you are afraid of leaving your house unattended. You work from home, so your house has all your work stuff in it as well as all your personal stuff. When you have to leave home overnight, you become consumed by fear that something bad is happening to it.

WISDOM: *A Buddha is someone who lives in peace, joy, and freedom, neither afraid of nor attached to anything. In this situation, letting go of your attachments can give you freedom and joy.*

SITUATION: After reading about a few burglaries in your area, you are thinking of installing an alarm system in your house. It is an added expense you just don't need now, but with two small children, you are afraid not to install the alarm system.

WISDOM: *Fear, anger, guilt, loneliness, and helplessness are all mental emotional responses that can intensify pain. The extra expense, if it offers some peace of mind, is worth it.*

SITUATION: Your intuition is telling you that refinancing your house so you can get a new kitchen is not a good idea. Your spouse really wants to get the new kitchen now, but you think that a bigger mortgage will set you back in your retirement plans. The mortgage broker says your house will increase in value because of the new kitchen, justifying the additional mortgage amount.

WISDOM: *As desires become fewer, frustration diminishes. What do you actually need?*

SITUATION: The mailbox at your house, along with the entire street's, was vandalized—by teenagers, you assume. All the mailboxes were hit with a baseball bat and toppled over. You are so angry that you just want to know who did it and see them punished.

WISDOM: *Revenge is an obstacle that will always interfere with happiness. When you are free of revenge, you can enjoy the wonders of life that are always available to you and experience lasting happiness.*

SITUATION: After 20 years of good use, your kitchen finally needs to be remodeled. You thought saving the money was going to be the hard part of this decision, but as it turns out, that was the easy part. There are so many products and designs to choose from, it is mind-boggling. You did not realize it would be so complicated.

WISDOM: *It is easy to get caught up in the small details and lose sight of the big picture. Genuine happiness lies in simplicity because simplicity brings more happiness than complexity. You don't need very much to be happy.*

SITUATION: How many clickers do you need to operate a television? It seems like your house is being filled with gadgets that are supposed to make things easier. You have gadgets for the kitchen, to listen to music, to exercise, and to be entertained. It seems complicated.

WISDOM: *Ask yourself, will this so-called convenience really simplify my life? Consciously choose voluntary simplicity that illuminates a basic and transforming truth: happiness does not depend on how much you have.*

SITUATION: It has come to your attention that the person you hired to mow your lawn and do landscaping work is an illegal immigrant. You are quite satisfied with the quality of work he does. He has always been reliable and honest in his work. It is very difficult to find workers who will do the tasks he does for the fee he charges.

WISDOM: *Appreciate the diversity of beings you encounter. Like flowers, they bring beauty, variety, and sustenance to your world.*

SITUATION: Long ago, you registered for the Do Not Call list to stop interruptions from telemarketers. Every day, violators of the Do Not Call Registry phone you. You try to ignore the calls or turn them in, but the calls just will not stop.

WISDOM: *Accept your anger. By doing so, you can transform it into positive energy.*

SITUATION: Recently, you tried to fix a minor plumbing leak in your house. You broke the pipe you were trying to fix and now have a big problem. You did not prepare for the task by first turning off the water in case something went wrong. By using common sense, you would have averted a major inconvenience, but instead you panicked.

WISDOM: *Like on an airplane, put on your oxygen mask first, then help others. This approach is based on being aware and paying attention. Take three deep breaths and then bring mindfulness to what is going on. Develop your concentration. Because you are fully in the present, you are naturally more calm and mindfully aware of the steps you are taking.*

SITUATION: It is difficult to save water in a house with two teenagers. Not only is water a precious natural resource, the electricity needed to heat the water for showers is, too. With your electric bill doubling since last year, you feel you need to take drastic action, especially since you are trying to save money for their college education.

WISDOM: *Try to teach your children that they are free in each moment to shape not only their own lives but also the world. What they plant, they will reap. If they can sacrifice a little and conserve water and other natural resources, they will benefit from it and so will others.*

SITUATION: Family members and friends laugh at your preparedness for emergency situations. All the cars in the house are equipped with bags of supplies. The house has a section filled with emergency rations. You feel more secure having supplies and a strategy developed to handle crisis situations efficiently.

WISDOM: *If there is preparation, there will be no regret.*

SITUATION: You live in an area that is prone to wildfires, but in the back of your mind, you think that such disasters happen to other people, not you. Unfortunately, it does happen to you. The police come through your neighborhood and give you 20 minutes to evacuate your house and gather a few items.

WISDOM: *What is important is clearly people and animals. Things can be replaced. Everything that seems so crucial eventually evaporates, like a dream. What is really important?*

SITUATION: To save money for your child's college fund, you and your spouse have decided to split the chore of cleaning the house instead of paying someone to do it for you. It is not your favorite thing to do, but you try to make the best of it.

WISDOM: *A clean house helps create a clear mind. Household chores, like cleaning, provide an excellent opportunity to practice mindfulness and self-discipline. Cleaning the house can be therapeutic. Think of your time cleaning as part of your exercise or as time to relax, decompress, and contemplate life. When you train yourself to look at housecleaning in a meditative way, you will see the work as rewarding and pleasant.*

SITUATION: Real estate and house-buying seem to be the only things your friends talk about. Many are buying houses themselves. You and your spouse are saving for a house but can't comfortably afford one yet. You feel a lot of pressure from everyone to buy a house.

WISDOM: *Waiting means patience and silence. It means not being driven to action by your desires. If you don't have the ability to wait, every desire that comes into your mind compels you to action, and you stay on board with the wheel of craving.*

SITUATION: A neighbor just put their house up for sale and is moving to a more desirable area of town. You are envious, jealous.

WISDOM: *Envy and jealousy stem from the fundamental inability to rejoice at someone else's happiness or success. Let go of these harmful feelings. They make your situation worse. Rejoice in others' happiness and you will have happiness.*

SITUATION: It seems like every house in the neighborhood is having some work done to it. At parties, the only thing people talk about is what they're having done to their houses and how complicated and chaotic it is.

WISDOM: *If we're not careful, we make our lives busy, chaotic, and complicated, filled with vacancy and meaninglessness. Our minds are confused by petty details and wants. Why are you even concerning yourself with what others are doing? Why compare?*

SITUATION: You cannot comfortably afford to move now, but you feel that by moving to a different town you will improve the quality of your life. The town you want to move to has so many more things to do than the town where you live now that you feel the risk is worth taking.

WISDOM: *You do not have to be in a special place to develop the love and compassion that improve the quality of your life. You can be anywhere.*

SITUATION: After saving for what seems like forever, you finally have enough money to make a down payment on a house. You found the house of your dreams and put a fair bid in for it based on what you could afford. Unfortunately, someone outbid you and got the house instead.

WISDOM: *Real blessings often appear in discouragement and disappointment.*

SITUATION: After house-hunting for a long time, you finally come across a house pretty close to your price range that has a magical feel to it.

WISDOM: *The wise have an inward sense of what is beautiful, and the highest wisdom is to trust this intuition and be guided by it. The answer to the last appeal of what is right lies within a man's own heart. Trust yourself.*

SITUATION: You are moving to a new, beautiful home—the house of your dreams. All the hard work over the years is finally paying off. Life is going to be great now.

WISDOM: *Not only does the object of our desire change over time, but our desires change too.*

Shopping

SITUATION: As you place the items in your shopping cart onto the self-checkout counter, you realize that you picked up something you don't really want. Instead of delaying your checkout process, you decide to leave the item to the side of the counter even though it will spoil without refrigeration.

WISDOM: *Be aware that your actions and inactions affect the whole world. Try not to be indifferent to the welfare of others. Open your heart to the universal caring that connects us all. Be careful, not careless.*

SITUATION: You cannot stand grocery shopping with your husband. Every time you cave in and take him along, your shopping cart fills up with items you don't really need. You try to stop him the best you can, but he does use his sad face very effectively, and you allow some silly stuff to be purchased.

WISDOM: *Whenever anger arises, recognize its transitory nature and respond with understanding instead of wrath.*

SITUATION: By accident, you are bumped into by someone's cart at the grocery store. You did not see this coming and you get upset.

WISDOM: *So, a grocery cart bangs into you at the store. You turn, see what has happened, move your cart out of the way, then turn your full attention back to shopping. The end. Do not add suffering or anger.*

SITUATION: You spend a lot of time researching flat-screen televisions before you purchase a new one. After a month, the television breaks. When you contact the company about repairs, the customer service representative is rude and unhelpful. Even when the television comes back from being repaired, it still does not work. After contacting the company again and still not getting the help you feel you deserve, your anger bursts out.

WISDOM: *Realize that anger is useless. It makes you unhappy. It makes a groove in the mind so that anger arises more and more easily.*

SITUATION: You purchase an expensive purse to take with you to a fancy event. The purse gets many compliments throughout the evening, yet the next day you decide you really did not want it and you return it.

WISDOM: *Quietly consider what is right and what is wrong. Right action is seeing things as they are instead of as you might prefer them to be.*

SITUATION: Even though your car is in fine condition, you've caught the new-car bug. The vehicle you really want is a lot more expensive than you thought, and you will have to take out a good-sized car loan to afford it. Yet you think that buying the new car will make you happier.

WISDOM: *Are you spending money just to acquire more things? To fulfill self-indulgent desires? Do you buy more than you can afford? By thinking that happiness consists of buying certain things, you burden yourself. If you live your life by waiting for some new object to own, happiness will always be just out of reach.*

SITUATION: After experiencing poor service on a purchase, you have a discussion with a friend on how these situations should best be handled. Do you get mad? Stop going to the place? Write a letter of complaint?

WISDOM: *Think about your own service. Consciously or unconsciously, every one of us does render some service or other. By cultivating the habit of doing your service with care and a smile, you will develop your happiness as well as that of others.*

SITUATION: Your best friend gets caught up with all the latest fads. She tries to convince you to join her, but you gracefully decline. You feel bad that she spends so much time, energy, and money chasing these fads, but you can't get through to her.

WISDOM: *Show your friend that you are trying to live in the present moment with the wisdom and awareness to renounce harmful actions, words, and thoughts. Maybe you can offer this: "Ask yourself if this will be important or even remembered in a month or a year. Ask yourself if this is useful or needed. Stopping to question your actions can help you overcome the habit of wanting."*

SITUATION: When restlessness sets in, you start to browse Internet shopping sites. You wonder why you can't concentrate on work.

WISDOM: *Restlessness, physical and mental, is a major distraction in life. You may be cognizant of physical restlessness, but not mental restlessness that leads to compulsive or obsessive behavior. Acknowledge that restlessness dissipates your energy and concentration. Let go of it by becoming aware and mindful in the moment.*

Money

SITUATION: Every time you purchase a lottery ticket, you have the same fantasy about how good life would be if you had a lot of money.

WISDOM: *It is only when we get beyond fantasy, beyond wishing and dreaming, that the real conversion takes place and we awaken reborn. Reality is the goal.*

SITUATION: In a million-to-one stroke of luck, you pick the winning numbers in the lottery. When your feet finally came back down to earth, you realize that being financially independent is rather complicated. It is a whole new world—and an adventure for you.

WISDOM: *Mindfully acknowledge the impermanence of satisfaction brought by objects of desire. Let go of all greed and cultivate desire only for experiences that lead you further along your spiritual path.*

SITUATION: You are dismayed and surprised at how many people go to the casino in your area. You are even more surprised at the amount of money they spend there. How can there be so many people willing to take chances with their money?

WISDOM: *Exactly why are you concerning yourself with this? Cultivate your own effort to pursue spiritual growth on the Middle Path. Cultivate your own moderation.*

SITUATION: A young and inexperienced cashier gave you too little change back at a fast-food restaurant during dinnertime when the restaurant was very crowded.

WISDOM: *Have the kindness to tolerate others' mistakes.*

SITUATION: At the bank ATM, extra money comes out that does not belong to you.

WISDOM: *Honesty brings peace.*

SITUATION: At the store, a cashier gave you change for a $20 instead of the $10 that you gave her.

WISDOM: *Any gesture of honesty will affect how you experience your world. What you do for yourself you also do for others, and what you do for others you do for yourself.*

SITUATION: Even though you and your spouse have good jobs with decent pay, it seems to be getting harder to pay the bills each month. You can't seem to get a handle on where your money goes. The stress is beginning to negatively affect the family dynamics.

WISDOM: *How much of the hard-earned money you make gets thrown away on the temporary pleasure of buying things that immediately become assimilated into your ever-growing collection of stuff? Do you work just to have more stuff?*

SITUATION: No matter how careful you are with money, it seems that the more you need, the less you have, and the more money you have, the more you need. This feeling leaves you a bit nervous and worried.

WISDOM: *In a world focused on material possessions, a balance between money and spiritual health can be achieved. Tame your "wanting mind" to achieve happiness and spiritual freedom. The wanting mind exists when you are not in the present moment and craves an experience different from the one you are currently having.*

SITUATION: Paying the bills at the end of the month, you always feel guilty when you come to the credit card statement. After matching up the receipts to the charges, you realize how many things you purchased that you did not need. You know all that money could have been used for a better purpose. But every month the same thing happens.

WISDOM: *When you are tempted to buy another pretty sweater even though your closet is full of them, discipline your mind. Replace the greedy thought with a generous one. Reflect mindfully on the impermanent nature of sweaters. If the mind is still whining and crying, you may need to give yourself an ultimatum. The mind learns to let go.*

SITUATION: Receiving your credit card bill after your vacation, you forget the enjoyment you had and feel the pain of paying for it.

WISDOM: *Happiness cannot be traveled to, owned, earned, worn, or consumed. Happiness is the spiritual experience of living every minute with love, grace, and gratitude. Enjoy the vacation by planning well for it.*

SITUATION: You knew not to get the new credit card, but you did anyway. Now your debt is above your means to pay it off.

WISDOM: *We don't receive wisdom; we must discover it for ourselves after a journey that no one can take for us or spare us.*

SITUATION: How did the credit card bill get so high? The minimum payments will take years to pay it off.

WISDOM: *It is better to pay and have a little less than to have much and be always in debt. It hurts to still be paying for something after the newness has worn off.*

SITUATION: You just got your credit card bill and are surprised to see it so high. You know that you've been using your credit card a little too often in the wake of a recent relationship breakup, but you did not realize that you'd gone that far overboard.

WISDOM: *Under anxiety, panic, distress, or depression, people sometimes reach for credit cards to relieve their pain. If you pay attention to what's true in the moment as you shop, that focused awareness will help cut through the compulsive habit of chasing desires and slow you down long enough to examine your habits.*

SITUATION: During this difficult economic time, you are grateful to have a job you feel fairly secure in. But, preparing for the worst, you are cutting back on many unnecessary material things. After a few months of lower credit card bills and more quality time with your family, you are realizing that you are actually happier than when you were eating out and going to stores all the time.

WISDOM: *Realize the joy and simplicity in being unencumbered by unnecessary possessions and incessant desires. When this effort is put forth, you experience a spaciousness and ease of mind, which comes from letting go of attachments.*

SITUATION: Economic times are tough, and there is talk of your firm merging with another company. To get yourself to sleep at night, you fantasize about what your life would be like if you won the lottery and had no more worries about money.

WISDOM: *Instead of running away from suffering by keeping yourself busy chasing after fantasies you think will bring happiness, make your spiritual work a priority. See how important and precious life is at the present moment, no matter what your situation is.*

SITUATION: Living paycheck to paycheck is no fun. Gas and food prices have skyrocketed so much that it is becoming difficult for you to keep up financially. You try not to live beyond your means, but inflation has set you back.

WISDOM: *All you need to be really happy is something to be enthusiastic about. All the happiness in the world comes from thinking of others. All the suffering in the world comes from thinking only of oneself.*

SITUATION: Keeping up with the Joneses is no easy task. Every party and every encounter with friends and neighbors ends up as a conversation about their new car or what they are having done to their house.

WISDOM: *Humans are so conditioned to want more that we burden ourselves with material acquisitions. Learning how to control, not be controlled by, your material desires is a giant step in getting control of your life. Let go of your attachments to things that don't last.*

SITUATION: It seems like you have become a little obsessed with thinking about your financial situation when you retire. From formulating strategies to reading about investment advice, more and more of your time is going into this endeavor.

WISDOM: *Moderation is the only way to find true balance, and it is the best way to live fully and with mindful awareness. What does obsession get you? It is like worry; it is a useless occupation.*

SITUATION: You are broke, but you just got a call from a friend whose car is being repaired, and he needs to borrow some money from you to get the car out of the shop.

WISDOM: *Wealth does not guarantee happiness. Wealth is impermanent. Those who understand this can find true happiness.*

SITUATION: A neighborhood child is coming to your house to ask for a donation for an upcoming charity walkathon. She's not the first one.

WISDOM: *Let yourself feel good about giving when you give, and take pleasure in reaching out and giving to others.*

SITUATION: After reading in the media about consumer and computer identity theft scams, you fear that someone will steal your identity and rack up bills that you will be responsible for.

WISDOM: *Stop training yourself to fear everything. Don't be guided by fear. Accept that no matter how you feel about it, life will never be predictable and orderly.*

SITUATION: On your way to work each morning, you pass a homeless man begging for money. You avoid making eye contact with him even though you feel badly for him. Seeing him changes a good mood into a sad one. Sometimes you even walk on the other side of the street so you do not have to look at him.

WISDOM: *True happiness can never be found through the avoidance of pain and suffering. It arrives when we understand that our own happiness is inextricably linked with the happiness of others. Every day is filled with opportunities to be generous. You cannot lose by being generous.*

SITUATION: During the economic good times, you rode the wave of prosperity. You were able to buy an expensive house and car. Going out to dinner was the norm, not a treat. All that changed when the economy went south and you lost your job. You realize that you were not very happy during the economic good times. You want your life to mean more than just being able to purchase things and experiences.

WISDOM: *Eliminate the conventional notion that a good life is about acquiring more and more material goods. Change to the idea that having a good life can be based on compassion and serving others.*

SITUATION: It is difficult for you to watch pro sports because of the ridiculously high salaries professional athletes make. The high price of admission to an athletic event reflects the athletes' salaries.

WISDOM: *Be free from judgment of others and yourself. Let it come and go without getting caught in it. Experience the dance of life without critical thoughts of how it should look.*

SITUATION: You just saw the worst movie ever. To top it off, it cost you $9 plus money for snacks. You wonder how they can get away with charging these prices for such a bad film.

WISDOM: *Become aware of the constant stream of judging and reacting in inner and outer experiences that you are caught up in, and step back from it. When such judgments dominate your mind, they make it difficult to find any peace within yourself.*

SITUATION: It is extremely important to you to be able to send both of your children through college debt-free. The sacrifices that you and your spouse are making to achieve this goal are great. You keep cars longer than you would like to. You eat more dinners at home to save money. You're making lots of little sacrifices to achieve an important goal.

WISDOM: *Anything worthwhile requires restraint and a certain amount of sacrifice. Making sacrifices to attain the greatest happiness is always better than going after trivial pleasure.*

SITUATION: At work recently, your boss forgot to bring money for lunch, so you lent him some money. It has been over a week and he has not paid you back. You are a little intimidated about asking him for the money back because he is your boss. He does not owe you a large sum, and it would be no big deal just to forget it, but it's the principle of the matter that is affecting you.

WISDOM: *What is the importance of this? Maybe he just forgot! There is space in your heart for generosity. Develop generosity at whatever level you find it arising in your heart. No one who is generous ever perishes from destitution.*

SITUATION: At tax time, it is your responsibility to take care of the family tax returns. You dread this responsibility because you hate numbers and you hate paying so much money toward taxes. But you are the only one in the family that is knowledgeable about taxes and good at organizing the information needed to fill out the tax returns.

WISDOM: *Cultivate the stability of a mountain, strengthened by the insight this viewpoint brings. Be strong while making a sacrifice.*

SITUATION: When you completed your income taxes this year, you took some liberal deductions to try to lower your payment. The deductions are probably not legitimate, but it will help you out financially as you struggle to make college tuition payments for your children.

WISDOM: *Commit to actions that help and do not harm. Do what you can to create a safe and good world for those around you, even as you work on your own spiritual transformation. Sow good seeds to reap good profits.*

SITUATION: After recently getting married, you and your spouse are beginning to save for your own place. To save the kind of money you need for a down payment, the two of you have to scale back big-time. When you were single, you never really had to worry about money, and life was pretty carefree. But now that you need to scale back on your expenses, it is pretty hard to do.

WISDOM: *Avoid extremes and mindfully choose moderation in all aspects of your life so that you can maintain the balance that supports spiritual transformation.*

SITUATION: During the housing boom, you refinanced your house so you could fix it up into your dream home. Now you are in a jam because the housing market crashed and your variable-rate mortgage has reset to a higher price—more than the value of the house. You cannot sleep at night worrying about how you are going to afford the higher mortgage payment.

WISDOM: *When you are completely overwhelmed by a problem, simply let your natural intelligence kick in by pausing and taking three deep breaths. Your natural intelligence is always there to help you find the right thing to do—as long as you don't ignore it.*

SITUATION: While your husband was alive, he did all the investing for your retirement. He enjoyed the challenge of figuring out where to invest the money and was good at it. Since your husband passed away, the responsibility for maintaining the investments and finances has fallen to you. You know that you will need to hire a financial adviser to help you, but you also want to gain enough knowledge so you are not taken advantage of.

WISDOM: *We all know more than we know we do.*

Others

SITUATION: Your best friend since kindergarten is moving to another state and you feel extremely sad about the situation.

WISDOM: *Great friendships last until the grave.*

SITUATION: A child is talking and talking and it's really getting on your nerves. The child clearly needs to talk, but you do not want to hear it.

WISDOM: *When someone needs to talk, be generous, listen carefully, offer compliments, and give accurate feedback.*

SITUATION: You can't pinpoint exactly when it started, but the older you get, the more intolerant you are of crying babies and whining small children. You find them quite annoying, especially when you are traveling. Your children are grown, and you can empathize with the parents, but the kids really annoy you now. You hope this changes when you have grandchildren.

WISDOM: *Be attuned to the nature of human life, which is common among all people of all ages. Mindfully use the recognition of this sameness to dispel notions of differences that might make anyone seem "other."*

SITUATION: One of your best friends said something unkind about another friend's actions. You are meeting the other friend tonight, and you're not sure whether to say anything about the incident.

WISDOM: *Wise speech is rooted in compassion and integrity, and it protects the people you speak to as well as your own heart from guilt and remorse.*

SITUATION: When you get home after going out with friends, you realize that something you said to one of them may have hurt her.

WISDOM: *Apologize immediately as soon as you recognize your lack of skill and mindfulness.*

SITUATION: You said something to hurt someone on purpose because you were angry with them. You were aware of what you were saying, but you still said it. The incident keeps circulating in your head.

WISDOM: *Transgressions are to be understood and corrected, not dwelt upon or agonized over.*

SITUATION: You are nervous going to your spouse's holiday party. You are not very confident in social situations and do not know many of the people your spouse works with. You are trying to make the evening successful and pleasant for your spouse.

WISDOM: *Become more aware of the room and the noises—or the silences between the noises.*

SITUATION: You are a little nervous about going to a party. The last time you went to a party with these same people, there was a lot of gossiping and talking about others who were not there. It made you uncomfortable.

WISDOM: *Be aware of what you are saying as you say it. Many people express their anxiety and discomfort in social situations through mindless speech. Remind yourself that when others ramble and prattle on without any real awareness of what they are saying, they are filling the void of their fear and anxiety with words.*

SITUATION: Having spent a lot of time and money planning a party at your house, you are a bit upset that some people haven't RSVPed yet. The party is only a week away, and you need to get a final count of how many people are coming so you can order the food and drinks.

WISDOM: *Anyone or anything that can make you angry is showing you how you let yourself be controlled by expectations of how someone or something should be.*

SITUATION: Invited to be in a friend's wedding party, you see the unflattering dress she has chosen for you to wear. She asks what you think of the dress.

WISDOM: *Each of us has experienced what happens when we do not communicate or when we have said something that was not true or genuine or beneficial. Relationships are weakened or disappear. Communication that is open, truthful, genuine, and compassionate creates a sense of communion.*

SITUATION: A neighbor is organizing a fundraiser for a family that has been hurt by an illness. In a family meeting, you discuss the best way to help out.

WISDOM: *Every time you think of helping someone else become more generous and giving, you plant powerful seeds within your own mind.*

SITUATION: A friend you grew up with lost her life in a terrible accident. You are still in touch with her family, and you decide to organize a fundraiser to establish a scholarship in her honor at the high school you both graduated from.

WISDOM: *Everyone can learn from your kindness, and everyone deserves your kindness.*

SITUATION: You live in a small town. Part of the success of a small town is reliant on how much time people volunteer to make it a better place to live. You have joined a committee that is suffering from terrible communication. Egos have clashed, and it is no longer about making the town a better place but instead about winning personal battles. Your goal is to change this atmosphere and have better communication so the town benefits.

WISDOM: *Improving communications within an organization is about developing better relationship skills through skillful speech and open listening. Communication of any kind can be improved when the people involved become better listeners, speak from the heart, and observe how they interact with each other.*

SITUATION: At the town meeting there is a major controversy surrounding the budget. The town is divided. About half the people support the budget and half don't. You are going to speak at the meeting because you feel strongly about your position.

WISDOM: *Before you speak, stop for a moment and think. Are you about to be helpful or harmful? Are you about to be skillful or unskillful? Are you about to be selfless or selfish? Are your words filled with loving kindness? Think kindly, speak gently and clearly.*

SITUATION: During a town hall meeting, you are asked to mediate between two parties who are arguing over ownership of a path that goes from the road to a boat launch.

WISDOM: *When you are capable of understanding and connecting your own experiences, then you can understand and connect to all people and life.*

SITUATION: You are running for a political office in your town. A reporter dug up some embarrassing dirt on you concerning an incident that happened more than 25 years ago and put it in an article in the local newspaper. You feel hurt and humiliated.

WISDOM: *The practice of forgiveness happens when you can realize the underlying cause of your anger and impatience. This allows you to distinguish between someone's unskillful behavior and essential goodness.*

SITUATION: A long time ago, someone very close to you hurt you very badly. You just found out that this person passed away.

WISDOM: *Forgiveness releases the grasp on pains of the past.*

SITUATION: You coach a children's sport team. Not all the coaches abide by the rule that all team members should get equal playing time. You are beginning to get some flack from other parents who want you to let the skilled players play more. You are not going to do that.

WISDOM: *Once you understand that the basic nature of humanity is compassionate rather than aggressive, your relationship to the world changes immediately. It helps you relax, trust, live at ease, and be happier. Be gentle, kind, thoughtful, caring, compassionate, loving, fair, responsible, and generous to everyone—including yourself.*

SITUATION: After witnessing outrageous behavior on the part of parents at a Little League game, you are seething with rage on the inside.

WISDOM: *When you become calm and serene on the inside, the world becomes more calm and serene on the outside.*

SITUATION: When you are walking and you encounter a person of a certain race, you automatically become suspicious of that person.

WISDOM: *Peace is most often found in the absence of prejudice.*

SITUATION: At an ATM one night, you are overcome by fear because someone of a different race gets in line behind you. You feel the blood rush to your head. You think for sure he is going to rob you. As you leave the ATM, the person behind you nods a hello to you. Now you feel bad that you were so suspicious.

WISDOM: *Become less judgmental about your fear. Begin to see how you are caught by fear, attachment, and aversion—the endless circle of seeking.*

SITUATION: It's moving day at your apartment. One of your friends does not show up to help you move as she promised she would.

WISDOM: *Don't dwell upon the faults of others. If you do, your own faults grow stronger.*

SITUATION: You've moved from your old house to a new house. While you lived in the old house, you were quite friendly with your neighbors. But now your old neighbors are no longer friendly to you.

WISDOM: *It is impossible to be happy and envious at the same time. If your old neighbors are not happy for you, then they were not really your friends.*

SITUATION: You have moved to a new town. Everyone seems like a stranger to you.

WISDOM: *Loving friendliness and a sense of interconnection with all beings and a sincere wish for them to be happy has far-reaching effects. Choose to be everybody's friend.*

SITUATION: After moving into a new neighborhood, you are having difficulty connecting with the other neighbors. This is not your strongest attribute to begin with, but it seems that all the friendships are in place and no one really wants to begin a new relationship.

WISDOM: *Not knowing how to touch the heart of another and forge loving, meaningful connections, you speak words that leave you isolated or frustrated. Use the power of words to build deeper connections. The connections you make with others, superficial or profound, most often begin with the spoken or written word.*

SITUATION: You've recently moved to a nice neighborhood in a nice town. It comes as a surprise to you that at every party you go to, the men and women separate into two separate groups, and everyone complains about their spouse. You were not expecting this type of behavior, and you're put off by it.

WISDOM: *Recognize that even the strongest emotions are temporary. They have power over a person for only as long as that person gives power to the emotions.*

SITUATION: You don't know why, but it appears one of your neighbors does not like you at all. You get the feeling that there is major hatred directed toward you.

WISDOM: *Live happily. Leave off hating, even as you live among those who hate. Hate has never yet dispelled hate. Only love dispels hate.*

SITUATION: You have met a group of people who you enjoy being with. However, some of their ideas and political beliefs are very different from yours. You wonder if it is possible to socialize with people who have a diversity of ideas and beliefs, even wrongheaded ones (in your opinion).

WISDOM: *Human nature allows us to consider valid those ideas that pass muster with our own particular tests and perceptions. It also shows us how difficult it is to agree with ideas that are outside these realms.*

SITUATION: In your neighborhood, there is one neighbor who gets on your nerves. It is difficult to deal with him because of the way he reacts toward you. You do not know why he acts like this.

WISDOM: *Deal with ill will toward someone who consistently treats you poorly and inappropriately by generating loving thoughts. Wish happiness and love to all beings everywhere, to individual people you feel kindly toward, and finally—even though it may be difficult—to the specific person you may be angry at.*

SITUATION: A friend of yours constantly blames other people when things do not go according to her plan. It is difficult for you to talk about this with her because then she gets mad at you.

WISDOM: *Your friend is responsible for the feelings and thoughts that arise in her. By blaming, she give up her capacity to choose. She gives up her freedom.*

SITUATION: While out one night, you saw a good friend's spouse out with another person, acting a little too friendly. Now you do not know what, if anything, to tell your friend.

WISDOM: *If you know anything that is helpful and true, find the right time. Do not speak impetuously. Think about it first, make sure that it will be helpful, that it's true, and that it's the right time. You'll know the right time has come when the other person is in a peaceful frame of mind and is agreeable to listening. It should be at a time when you have loving feelings for that person.*

SITUATION: You considered yourself a "people person" until recently. Now it seems that you get mad and irritated at people easily. Whether family or coworkers, it seems everyone is making you angry.

WISDOM: *When you say someone has made you angry, you are not acknowledging that the seed of anger is inside you, that the other person simply touched that seed and set your own anger going. Realizing this can help you restore control to your mind and see your correct relationship with those around you.*

SITUATION: You are telling a personal secret to your best friend. You know she will not tell anyone else.

WISDOM: *Next time you talk to your best friend, relish the pauses and also the trust flowing within the conversation.*

SITUATION: When you first meet someone new, you almost always forget the person's name. It is embarrassing when you see this person again and can't remember their name.

WISDOM: *Listening is an art. Listen with a still and concentrated mind. Then it is possible to be responsive to what is being said.*

SITUATION: You read in the local newspaper that a fellow classmate and friend of yours passed away. The news makes you very sad.

WISDOM: *The key to your peace of mind lies not in your circumstances, but in how you respond to them. Meditation gives you an opportunity to cultivate acceptance for things as they are. Life is painful; suffering is optional.*

SITUATION: Your college roommate is constantly getting involved with romantic relationships to feel worthwhile. You get the feeling that many of the people she gets involved with are taking advantage of her, and her self-esteem is still pretty low.

WISDOM: *You can help her discover the wisdom of ceasing to externalize the source of happiness and reclaiming her capacity to nurture inner well-being and wholeness.*

SITUATION: You met a new friend recently and felt an instant connection with him. You enjoy spending time with this person because he seems to be able to look at life in a very refreshing way, as if everything is new to him.

WISDOM: *"Beginner's Mind" is a mind that is willing to see everything as if for the first time.*

SITUATION: A friend was supposed to get tickets to a show that you really want to see. After showing up late to the meeting place, he informs you that he was not able to get the tickets.

WISDOM: *When there's disappointment, it may be the beginning of a great adventure.*

SITUATION: A neighbor is asking you for another favor—again. She is a single mother trying to raise two children. Lately, it seems like she is asking you to watch her children too frequently.

WISDOM: *Bestow a favor, then forget it.*

SITUATION: A friend is re-marrying his ex-wife. Being familiar with the history of why the marriage did not work out the first time, you wonder if you should say something to them.

WISDOM: *Often we hold friends by holding our tongues. A still tongue keeps a wise head.*

SITUATION: Punctuality is not one of your strongest traits. You don't know where the time goes, but you are late to most events.

WISDOM: *Get ready to go on time so you don't delay others. Good actions create good consequences, and wasted time means you are not going forward. Remember, though, that if you hurry, you waste precious time—the time for being alive.*

SITUATION: Having reached a new stage of your life—marriage, career, kids—you just do not have as much time to hang out with close friends. One of them does not understand this and gets angry when you have to say "no" to going out with her. It has nothing to do with disliking her. It is strictly a time issue. Other things compete for your attention.

WISDOM: *Angry comments by someone are usually requests for more attention. When you are subjected to angry speech, you can usually end the situation by listening—really listening—instead of reacting.*

SITUATION: You are going to a movie because everyone you know has seen it and is talking about it, even though you know it is very graphic and filled with bad language.

WISDOM: *When you know something is not wholesome, let go of it. Watch uplifting movies.*

SITUATION: You are in a mentoring program in your city. One of the people you are mentoring is a former prostitute. It is challenging to work with her because her life is so drastically different from yours.

WISDOM: *Through mindfulness, compassion, and kindness toward those who create or once created suffering, you help generate conditions of happiness for them and yourself.*

SITUATION: After seeing a movie about a homeless person, you become inspired to do something for the unfortunate.

WISDOM: *The person who has no compassion can never be happy. The moment compassion is born in you, you feel better. When you look at all beings with eyes of love and compassion, you feel wonderful!*

SITUATION: Recently, some teenagers in your town committed a hate crime. The crime appalled you, but one of the teenagers who committed the crime is friends with your son.

WISDOM: *Every attitude you have toward another person is an attitude you have toward yourself. If you hate someone, it is because you hate those same feelings or tendencies in yourself. If you judge someone, it is because you judge yourself in the same way.*

SITUATION: Your best friend just announced that she is getting married— and to a really nice guy.

WISDOM: *The more you are concerned about the happiness of others, the more you build your own happiness at the same time. Do not expect anything in return. Think only of what is good for the other person.*

SITUATION: A friend of yours is famous, but he loves his privacy. Someone knows you're friends with this celebrity and has asked you to ask him to help out with a fundraiser.

WISDOM: *See what is. Acknowledge it without judging it as right or wrong. Let it go and come back to the present moment.*

SITUATION: You know someone who is thinking of joining the National Rifle Association.

WISDOM: *Guns may not hurt people, but they sure don't help. Guns support violence, and trading in weaponry is an unskillful livelihood.*

SITUATION: A next-door neighbor sure seems to enjoy himself a lot. Almost every weekend he has a loud party that goes well into the evening.

WISDOM: *When you complain about your neighbor's faults, count ten of your own.*

SITUATION: You enjoy attending church, and you want to become a little more involved in the spiritual aspect of your life.

WISDOM: *Form your own prayer group, especially if you belong to a church or synagogue or if you are taking a yoga or meditation class. You are sure to find other people who will also be interested in a prayer group.*

SITUATION: You are the one everyone goes to for solace when they are hurt and suffering. Sometimes it feels like you just don't have the strength to help others all the time.

WISDOM: *Actions that are kind, unselfish, and virtuous, which relieve suffering in others, help you accumulate good karma. They are an expression of wisdom, higher sanity, and enlightenment.*

SITUATION: A friend of yours calls you briefly about a lofty goal she has set for herself. She needs some help in defining her goal and setting up a plan, and she wants to get together with you to talk about it in more detail.

WISDOM: *When someone tells you about their goal, point out possibilities, not obstacles.*

SITUATION: At the time, you thought a practical joke you played was funny. But upon further review, you realize that it was mean and hurtful. People you know and like were hurt because of your action.

WISDOM: *When you've acted badly or inappropriately, note how your actions affected the other people involved. Take full responsibility, even though others may have participated, and become determined not to repeat the actions. Breathe in the responsibility, pain, and other negative emotions involved. Breathe out forgiveness, understanding, and compassion.*

SITUATION: Someone you know claims to practice "right speech." You have to admit that you find them to be honest. But sometimes in their quest for honesty, they say things that hurt people.

WISDOM: *In right speech, we adhere to making our words be true, kind, and helpful. If you know someone who speaks truthfully and honestly, realize that is wonderful, though it can also be painful. Although it is possible to say what is true and not be helpful at all, it is much better for speech to be both true and helpful.*

SITUATION: You did not even realize it until someone brought it to your attention, but every time you are walking in the city and you see someone of a different race from you, you clutch your purse tightly.

WISDOM: *Become mindful of everything you think, and learn to change it from unwholesome to wholesome.*

SITUATION: It has always been hard for you to accept yourself and others. Since you were young, you have never felt that you were worthy of good things. This negativity has affected how you relate to other people and increased the difficulty you have developing friendships.

WISDOM: *If you cannot accept yourself and treat yourself with kindness, you cannot do this for another person. Make friends with yourself. Then you will be making friends with others.*

SITUATION: At school, you overheard a racial remark that was about you. You thought the person who said it liked you. It kind of floored you before it made you angry. You've never looked at your relationships with your fellow students in a racial way. Now your emotions are all confused.

WISDOM: *People never stop saying and doing the wrong things, but it doesn't matter. The only thing that matters is peace and happiness in your own heart.*

SITUATION: You are a conversation junkie in need of a fix. It seems like you are always talking or making some noise. Never a silent moment in your life. Never silence in which to reflect on things. It almost seems as if you are afraid of what happens when there is silence.

WISDOM: *Reflect on all the times you've opened your mouth and spoken for no reason at all—out of habit, to fill a silence. Idle speech is meaningless speech used to fill in gaps when you are afraid of silence. It is speech that has no purpose. It is beautiful and peaceful to stay in a place of silence of mind. Discover the blessing of inner silence and peace. Speak mindfully and listen for interconnectedness between yourself and others.*

SITUATION: You misread the party invitation as saying "informal" when it said "formal." You arrived at the party in jeans, only to find that everyone else was dressed in evening gowns and tuxedos. You were the talk of the party, of course.

WISDOM: *In every situation where you feel discomfort, it is because you want something to be different. You're grasping at an idea about the way reality should be, instead of simply being present for what is. Reality is not passive acceptance, but being aware of what really is in this moment.*

SITUATION: When you were out with some friends, one of them put you down, saying something nasty about you. It was a lousy thing for the friend to say, and it hurt you tremendously. After a few days, the friend tried to apologize to you, but you wanted nothing to do with her.

WISDOM: *When one word has the power to make you hot and angry, why should not another word have the power to heal?*

SITUATION: Walking out of the water toward your friends on the beach, your bathing suit decides to do something weird on you. It is embarrassing, and you are worried what your friends will think.

WISDOM: *The Zen approach to worry is simple: just don't do it. No matter how much you worry or fret over something, it never helps the situation.*

SITUATION: During a performance by your choir, you were so into the singing that you started to sing an extra verse after everyone else stopped. It was quite embarrassing.

WISDOM: *Laugh when you let yourself get caught up in something small.*

SITUATION: While attending a friend's wedding reception, you take a spill on the dance floor and feel embarrassed. You'd had a little too much to drink and gotten a little crazy on the dance floor, resulting in the funny falling episode. The worst part is that the camera was rolling and got the whole thing on film. The only thing you can think of is that it is going to be submitted to one of those "funniest home video" shows or turn up on YouTube.

WISDOM: *When embarrassed, stop talking and thinking about it and move on to something else.*

SITUATION: You go to a movie with some friends. When you are all discussing it afterward, someone repeats a joke that was in the movie. Everyone laughs, but you don't get it. You feel really stupid and embarrassed because someone has to explain it to you.

WISDOM: *Emotions are a part of our lives. When you calmly investigate the emotions that spring up in us, you see that they are impermanent. They come and go.*

SITUATION: At your high school reunion, someone you knew from elementary school blurts out an old nickname that was embarrassing and hurtful to you when you were growing up.

WISDOM: *Do not throw insults back or get angry with the insults or bad talk of others, even though they insult you. Laugh and ignore attempts to provoke you.*

SITUATION: While working out at the gym, you sense a clothing item inching its way up, causing an itch. It's driving you crazy, so you scratch it for relief. While scratching, you notice that you are being watched.

WISDOM: *Sometimes we develop an itch in a private place. Scratch away.*

SITUATION: At a neighborhood house party, you have an emergency bathroom situation and forget to lock the door. As you're doing your business, a neighborhood kid walks in on you. It is extremely embarrassing for you as well as the kid.

WISDOM: *Relax, lighten up, and laugh. It's all funny.*

SITUATION: After your divorce, you lost a lot of confidence and self-esteem. You can handle this when you are alone, but when you are in a social setting, it is difficult to deal with.

WISDOM: *When you are at ease with yourself in social situations, you have the stability and confidence to handle anything that happens. You will not find yourself waiting to see how people react to you or what they say or think about you.*

SITUATION: In social situations, you seem to panic and talk so much that you do not even know what you're saying. You realize by the looks on people's faces that you are just rambling, but you don't seem to be able to control it.

WISDOM: *Many of us express our anxiety and discomfort in social situations through mindless speech. We ramble and prattle on without any real awareness of what we are saying. We are filling up space, filling the void of our fear and anxiety with words. To eliminate unskillful states, simply be aware of the moment.*

SITUATION: You lose your best friend because of something you said. This loss pains you to no end. You have tried to apologize, but your friend does not want to hear about it.

WISDOM: *Speech is very powerful. When it is truthful, honest, genuine, and beneficial, it builds harmony with friends. The five characteristics of well-spoken words are: spoken at the proper time, spoken in line with the truth, spoken beneficially, spoken gently, and spoken with a friendly heart.*

SITUATION: A group of your friends are thinking about getting tattoos. You really do not want to put something permanent on your body, and you know it will hurt your parents, but your friends are all getting them.

WISDOM: *People have a natural tendency, regardless of their personality traits, to automatically and mindlessly start thinking, feeling, and acting like the people around them. If you find yourself in a group with people who are doing things you do not believe to be good, leave at once. Try to avoid them as much as possible.*

SITUATION: Although you are heterosexual, one of your best friends is homosexual. While not agreeing 100 percent with his lifestyle, you still love him and enjoy his company. When you go out with him, you are amazed by all the harassment he endures. He tells you that sometimes at work it is even worse.

WISDOM: *All the energies of anger, hatred, fear, and violence come from wrong perceptions. When you are the target, you may start to feel anger, hatred, and fear, too. It is healthier to let it go; let it be their problem.*

SITUATION: During the 9/11 terrorist attacks, one of your oldest friends lost her life. You had known this friend since you were three years old. Not a day goes by that you don't think about your friend, get angry that this happened, and worry about future terrorist acts.

WISDOM: *Living in anger and fear is one of the worst things that can happen to you. For starters, unlearn anger and fear. When you overcome anger, you will be successful in controlling and letting go of fear, and calm will arise.*

SITUATION: Things are going really well for you at this stage of your life. You want to give something back by volunteering your time with an organization that helps people.

WISDOM: *When intensively generating goodwill and loving kindness, you create an extreme state of well-being. The more fully you give your energy, the more it returns to you.*

SITUATION: You are proud of your ethnic background, and you're planning a dinner party with some friends so you can share your cultural heritage with others.

WISDOM: *Take time to wag your tail a little.*

SITUATION: A very old friend is better at communicating by email than in person or on the phone. Sometimes you get very long emails telling you about her problems. You are more of a people person than an email person, and reading the emails is just not the same as listening to a friend talk to you.

WISDOM: *There is great skill involved in learning how to listen. Courtesy is most precious. Be open and accepting of others.*

SITUATION: A friend of yours gave your email address to someone whom you did not want to have it. Now you are getting annoying and inappropriate emails from this person. You are pretty upset that your friend gave out your address.

WISDOM: *If you are angry and speak harshly to another, you lose your spiritual footing and create pain, causing the other's mind to become disturbed and upset. Find ways to keep your words gentle, loving, accurate, and positive—even when you are annoyed or upset.*

SITUATION: You are not yet 21 years of age, but a bunch of your friends, who are also under 21, are going to a bar. They all have fake IDs and they can get you one, too.

WISDOM: *We often look for fulfillment and satisfaction in the wrong places. It is often better to do nothing than to do what is wrong.*

SITUATION: When you go on your daily walk, you're bothered when people stop and ask you questions. If one more person from out of town asks you directions to get to the center of town, you are just going to scream. Why can't these people get adequate directions before they leave their homes?

WISDOM: *Let your kindness rain on all. Be kind to people you do not know and try to look into their eyes' and hearts' warmth.*

SITUATION: During a big snowstorm, the snowplows that cleared your street missed part of the cul-de-sac. You have written and called the mayor to complain about the terrible job that was done.

WISDOM: *When you take the path of complaining, each complaint lays the ground for the next complaint, and nothing gets any better. Complaining is the byproduct of an untamed mind. What is the point of complaining or criticizing? A clearer, more direct request or suggestion may help alleviate a problem.*

SITUATION: This is your first time babysitting for new neighbors. Not only do you want to make a good impression for future babysitting opportunities, you also want to make a good impression with the newcomers. The children you are babysitting have gone through a lot of changes in the move and are pretty rambunctious. You are trying many things to get them under control and yet have them enjoy themselves, but nothing seems to work.

WISDOM: *Maybe what you tried didn't work. Great! Now you know something that doesn't work, and you can try something else that might work a lot better.*

SITUATION: A neighborhood friend has promised several times to call you so the two of you can get together. Unfortunately, she never calls. Every time you see her in the neighborhood, you feel angry and embarrassed. You're not sure what to do. You have no idea why she will not call you or return your calls.

WISDOM: *Let go of anger by staying in the present moment. Let the anger flow in and then out instead of blocking it and keeping it in. Accept anger with genuine loving kindness and then let it go. If you suppress it, the attachment nurtures its roots. It's okay to let it come and let it go.*

SITUATION: At a sporting event at a rival high school, you observe some students from that school interacting positively with students who obviously have mental and physical disabilities. Even though the team is your competition, you feel so good after seeing these students interacting with each other in such a natural state that you decide to write their principal a letter expressing how good you felt.

WISDOM: *Words have the power to destroy or heal. When words are both true and kind, they can change the world.*

SITUATION: You thought that being teased or picked on only happened to children. But a certain neighbor is relentless with his teasing. Whenever he discovers something about you, you become his prey, and the teasing begins. You feel so inferior when that happens.

WISDOM: *"The fool thinks he has won a battle when he bullies with harsh speech, but knowing how to be forbearing alone makes one victorious."*
—Samyutta Nikaya

SITUATION: Since you began your meditation practice last year, you have noticed a strange thing happening with your friends and co-workers. It seems like they respect you more than they did before. It is hard to explain, but they seem to be coming to you for advice and companionship more than they did before you began your practice.

WISDOM: *When you truly love yourself, you begin to know yourself better and realize what good you are capable of doing. It usually turns out that you are capable of much more than you usually dare to let yourself imagine.*

SITUATION: There is someone in your yoga class whom you just don't understand. Everyone else in the class is friendly and helpful except this one person. She never has a smile on her face or a nice word to say.

WISDOM: *When you let wisdom and compassion work together, you can begin to understand the nature of another person and can balance your feelings of empathy and commiseration successfully.*

SITUATION: A good friend of yours is always exaggerating her stories so she appears superior to everyone else. When you try to tell a story, she always comes up with a similar, better story. It is beginning to get on your nerves.

WISDOM: *Feeling superior to someone else, whether physically, intellectually, in stature, or in achievements, will always produce the same result: suffering. Your ability to feel compassion and to listen deeply are distorted because you are so convinced of the truth of your own views and opinions.*

SITUATION: Lately, one of your friends has been mean to people in your circle. Everyone, including you, is really mad at her for the way she is treating people. You suspect that her change in personality is due to a recent breakup with her boyfriend, but in your opinion there is still no reason to take it out on friends.

WISDOM: *Only an unhappy person acts in a nasty and mean way. A happy person acts and speaks in a happy way and will not make others angry. The person you are so angry with is suffering, experiencing unhappiness. Have some compassion for her suffering.*

SITUATION: Whenever you see a certain acquaintance at social activities in your neighborhood and town, she comes up to you and will not give you any space the rest of the time you are there. No matter how politely you try to remove yourself from her company, it doesn't work.

WISDOM: *Getting away from people whom you find distracting or annoying does not solve all your problems. Learn to work with these feelings in yourself and create a balance, because relationships provide you with opportunities.*

SITUATION: You are tired of having meaningless conversations, talking just for the sake of talking. No one can remember what was said or why it was said. You want to find ways to start conversations that have deeper meaning.

WISDOM: *Think about how you would prefer to have a conversation. When you practice mindful speech and deep listening, you can help make your conversations deeper, more meaningful, and more satisfying.*

SITUATION: Your cell phone is always on and always ringing. When you look at your bill, you are amazed at how many minutes you spend on the phone each month. Most of the conversations you have are nonessential— just talk for the sake of talking. Often, after these conversations, you feel bad because you engaged in gossiping or negative speech about someone.

WISDOM: *When you have a strong habit of talking too much and your speech does not serve you or the people you are talking to well, make a conscious effort to restrain yourself. So much time in our lives is spent talking, discussing, and gossiping about unimportant or irrelevant things that it does not serve us or the people we are talking to in a positive way.*

SITUATION: You have recently retired and are excited about all the opportunities that await you. Upon reflecting on how generous life has been to you, you decide that you would like to give back to society and people less fortunate than you. Your first volunteer adventure is to drive cancer patients who have no mode of transportation to their hospital and doctor visits.

WISDOM: *If you want to be happy for life, help somebody else who is hurting more than you, because nothing can erase your good deeds.*

SITUATION: You were a Big Sister during your college years and enjoyed the experience immensely. You stayed in touch with your Little Sister well past college and feel that you had a positive impact on her life. Now that your children are grown and on their own, you are thinking of becoming a Big Sister again.

WISDOM: *To gain wisdom, happiness, self-control, mindfulness, and other positive traits, a necessary ingredient is exposure to role models who have already developed wisdom, happiness, self-control, mindfulness, and other positive traits. People cannot achieve character development alone because we are connected and interdependent with each other. It truly does take a village.*

SITUATION: A local therapeutic horse-training facility for disabled people is facing a difficult financial situation. You were recently at a social gathering and someone associated with the organization asked you if you could help them out in some way. You believe in the organization and what they are trying to do, but you know it will take more than just you to get the job done.

WISDOM: *A common cause and vision of what is possible, shared by a group of people, fosters change and growth. Working together as a community can solve many problems.*

SITUATION: Although you consider yourself a pretty nice person, whenever you see someone trip or fall, you laugh inside. Even if the person who falls gets hurt, your first reaction is to laugh.

WISDOM: *Love, laugh, delight, and hold onto nothing.*

SITUATION: You try not to criticize how people look or the clothes they wear, but at a recent beach outing with friends, you couldn't help making fun of people who were wearing bathing suits they should not have been wearing.

WISDOM: *Use the gift of vision to recognize without discrimination the ingredients of your world. Be mindful about imposing good and bad attributes upon what you see.*

SITUATION: You have a giving soul. You are at your happiest when you can help out and nurture others. It appears as if you are sacrificing to help and nurture others, but in fact this is not the case. You derive so much pleasure and satisfaction from helping and nurturing others that you almost feel selfish and guilty.

WISDOM: *Giving openheartedly of your time, energy, material objects, kindness, care, and love helps you see your expectation of response. Happiness, freedom, and peace of mind are attained by giving them to someone else.*

SITUATION: A good friend of yours has a habit of cursing a lot. She has used foul language for as long as you can remember. When you were younger, you got a kick out of the shock value of her speech. But now that you have children, you do not want them exposed to it.

WISDOM: *Even when spoken out of habit, abusive language fuels anger in oneself and others. Harsh language that is habitual, like profanity, is mindless. Your friend can unlearn this habit. When she becomes aware of what she is saying and wants to change it, she will.*

SITUATION: Late one night, your neighbor called you, shaken and frightened to go into her house because it was clear her house had been burglarized.

WISDOM: *Try to let go of your fears and projections and see the simple truth of each moment. Understanding and wise responsiveness manifest in your speech, actions, and choices.*

SITUATION: You felt the bump in the crowd of people, but you did not realize that your wallet was taken from your back pocket until it was too late to see who did it. The wallet contained money, credit cards, and personal information. You feel violated that someone did this to you.

WISDOM: *An innocent person should not feel the need to punish a guilty person, because the guilty person punishes himself through the principle of karma. It takes true wisdom to be patient, and it may take a long time, but eventually all things will come around and pass.*

SITUATION: You were in a convenience store when it was held up by someone with a gun. You don't think you have ever been more frightened in your life. The event seemed surreal. You keep on replaying it over and over in your brain. Luckily, the employee handed over the money to the crook, who bolted away with no further incident. Now you look at life in a whole different light. It seems a lot more valuable now than it did before the crime.

WISDOM: *When you begin to understand the value and importance of life, you no longer want to waste time. Your choices and priorities change to reflect your newfound wisdom.*

SITUATION: You were a lifeguard in college, and you still remember some lifesaving techniques. While out one evening, you witness someone apparently having a heart attack. You immediately call 911 and begin administering CPR.

WISDOM: *In a crisis situation, you have the responsibility and power to take action. Do not doubt yourself, lose hope, or remain passive. Just do the best you can under the circumstances. Doing something is better than doing nothing.*

SITUATION: Since you were young, you have had a love affair with books. The way a book can take you to a different place and time is one of the most exciting things you have ever experienced. Reading has always been a solitary pastime, but now a good friend who is starting up a book club asks if you wanted to join. It will mean you'll have to participate in discussion about the books you read. What was once a solitary joy will now be a group event.

WISDOM: *Share the best of yourself—your joy, your love—through your words. Try to avoid sharing the worst of yourself—blaming, criticizing, judgmental words. Use your words to support, not tear down.*

SITUATION: A friend reads her horoscope every day and tells you how accurate it is. Now she wants you to go to a fortune teller with her. You are skeptical about horoscopes and fortune telling.

WISDOM: *It is more important to have wisdom than psychic powers. Even if psychic powers exist, they tend to lead us away from what is really important and valuable in life, like loving kindness and wisdom. Psychic abilities do not guarantee the wisdom to use them properly. It is better to turn away from people who think they can predict the future. Use your energies and time leading a more loving and wise life.*

SITUATION: If you don't write something down, you forget it. There is so much going on in your life, both professionally and personally, that it is difficult to keep track of everything. While you try to write down all the important things so you can keep track of them, sometimes you forget, and it causes scheduling conflicts. You would like to remember things better.

WISDOM: *Trying to change, thinking you have to do something about how and who you are, comes mostly from a sense of unworthiness and personal distrust. Give this feeling space, becoming aware of it without judging it. Always try to see yourself through God's eyes.*

SITUATION: While running for exercise, one of your neighbors, a friend, suffered a heart attack and passed away, leaving behind a wife and two small children. You are having trouble coping with the tragedy; you can't imagine how your friend's family is holding up.

WISDOM: *One way to alleviate the negative feelings from dealing with a tragedy is to help out the person most affected by the tragedy.*

SITUATION: Lately, a question has been on your mind: Is life random, or is it predestined? Someone in your condo who was the picture of perfect health died from a massive heart attack at a young age. You used to see this person running, riding a bike, or swimming all the time. The incident is causing you to reflect on whether life is random or not.

WISDOM: *Awareness, insight, and health ripen on their own if you are willing to pay attention in the moment and remember that you have only moments to live.*

SITUATION: Having heard a funny, off-color joke the other day, you decide to retell it to some people. The joke makes fun of a particular racial stereotype. When you tell it to one person who you didn't realize had some of this race in their ancestry, she doesn't find it funny. You apologize, and she accepts your apology, but you still feel guilty for having told the joke.

WISDOM: *It is a temptation to show how clever or funny you are by poking fun at someone or something, but it can be hurtful even in the guise of a joke.*

SITUATION: Making friends has never been a problem in your life. Making good friends, however, is. It seems you attract people who can easily lead you astray, and you wind up doing things that you later regret.

WISDOM: *Whether it is easy or hard for you to make friends, choose friends who are stable and can be relied upon. Good and trusting friends are a main ingredient for a happy and successful life.*

SITUATION: When you were growing up, there was a mentally disabled girl in your neighborhood. Although you were brought up to know it was wrong, sometimes you and your friends, as a group, would tease and make fun of her. At the time, you all thought it was funny, but it is something you wish you had never done and would like forgiveness for.

WISDOM: *We all do things we regret and want forgiveness for. When we recognize transgressions and repent with an open heart, we increase our happiness and goodness. Just as we forgive others, we must learn to forgive ourselves. We may not be able to change the past, but we can sure learn from it.*

SITUATION: At a silent-auction fundraiser at the local library, a portrait painting is up for bid. You've always wanted to have a painted portrait of your children, so after figuring how much it is worth to you, you make a bid. One of your neighbors places a higher one, and the next thing you know, you're in a bidding war—which you win. Afterward, you hear that your neighbor is a little upset with you because she really wanted the portrait. The fundraiser was for a good cause, and you feel you did nothing wrong.

WISDOM: *We all see life through different eyes because there are various ways to see the same thing. How you see it depends on your perception at a particular time and place.*

SITUATION: You spread a bad and untrue rumor about a former friend because you are angry with her. Now you wish you could take back what you said; you actually feel dirty for saying it.

WISDOM: *Whenever you have completed saying something, ask yourself whether what you have said resulted in well-being or harm to yourself or others. If you answer "well-being," stay mentally refreshed and joyful. If you answer "harm," resolve never to make this mistake again.*

SITUATION: Your children's nanny is trying to become a United States citizen, but it's not easy. You can't believe the frustration of all the red tape she has to deal with. In your mind, she is the kind of person whom the United States should want as a citizen: she loves the country and is hard working, loyal, and productive.

WISDOM: *With joy and gratitude, see the beauty of yourself and others. We reflect and are reflected in the radiance of each other, all in the sacred web of the world.*

SITUATION: A friend whom you have known for a long, long time has recently had a run of bad luck. When you called her the other day, you could not believe how depressed and negative her voice sounded on her answering machine. You want to advise her that she should cheer up her message a little because it may help improve her outlook.

WISDOM: *Find the blessing of inner silence and peace. This will help you mindfully speak to and listen for the interconnectedness between you and others. Maybe you can teach your friend the amazing tool of being able to just let things go, avoiding the grip of angry, passionate, worried, or depressed thoughts.*

SITUATION: At your wedding, you receive a nice, thoughtful (and expensive) gift from a relative, but it does not match your taste. You store it in the attic, not knowing what else to do with it. One day while cleaning out the attic, you notice the gift. As it happens, you're invited to a friend's new housewarming party, and the gift would be perfect for their home. You're sure no one will ever find out what you are doing; you decide to re-gift the present.

WISDOM: *By mindfully taking responsibility for and modifying hurtful intentions before they become actions, you will recognize and remember that you have the potential for transformation. If you feel that your planned action is harmful, refrain from doing it.*

Boy Meets Girl

SITUATION: You have been using an Internet social network to meet people to date. You thought you found a really nice person whom you wanted to get to know better. But it turns out he was just leading you on for fun and you were the butt of a joke. You are feeling very hurt and vulnerable.

WISDOM: *Someone who seeks happiness by hurting others who seek happiness will never find happiness. Instead of holding firmly to something that keeps you stuck in hurt, just let go and forgive those who have hurt you. This will release you from a great burden of unhappiness.*

SITUATION: You go out on a first date with someone and experience the weirdest déjà vu ever. You swear that you've met this person before. But there's no way you two could have met—you're from different parts of the country. It is very real to you, and you can't explain it.

WISDOM: *Through the endless cycles of birth, death, and rebirth, all of us are related.*

SITUATION: You have a movie date to see a film from a genre you cannot stand and then to eat at your least favorite restaurant, but these are your partner's favorites.

WISDOM: *We are very often driven by our likes and dislikes, totally unaware of the tyranny of our own thoughts and the self-destructive behaviors that often result from them.*

SITUATION: The love of your life wants to be a friend and not a lover.

WISDOM: *A relationship free of unrealistic grasping is free of disappointment, conflict, and jealousy. There is no freedom in holding onto someone who does not want to be held.*

SITUATION: After a nasty breakup with a boyfriend, you find yourself in a new relationship that's moving a bit faster than you would like, but you don't seem to be able to slow down.

WISDOM: *We usually act out of habit. The more you can get in touch with your motivations, the more likely you are to act in ways that are in harmony with your deepest values.*

SITUATION: When you were younger, someone did not respect your wishes to stop during a sexual encounter. You never pursued the matter, but it has caused you some suffering later on in life.

WISDOM: *Think, "There are many ways I have been wounded and hurt, abused, and abandoned by others in thought, word, or deed, knowingly or unknowingly. In the many ways others have hurt or harmed me, out of fear, pain, confusion, or anger, I see these now. To the extent I am ready, I offer them forgiveness. I have carried this pain in my heart too long. For this reason, to those who have caused me harm, I offer you my forgiveness."*

SITUATION: Your relationship with a boyfriend is not headed in a healthy direction. You have kept this bottled up and feel like you are going to explode if it continues much longer.

WISDOM: *Always try to be open with others so that they will be open with you.*

SITUATION: You just discovered that your boyfriend has been cheating on you. You knew that the two of you were having some problems in the relationship, but you thought it was something you could resolve. Your heart is broken. You thought this relationship had a chance to go to the next level. You feel so hurt now that it is unbearable. You just can't understand why someone would do this to another person.

WISDOM: *When you become aware of what is going on in your mind and body, you develop endurance and patience so that you may be able to observe and experience both painful and pleasurable events. You will respond more reasonably if you train your mind to be calm.*

SITUATION: Getting your hair cut before the prom does not go according to plan. Your hair does not come out the way you wanted or expected. There is nothing you can do about it now. There is no more time left to get ready. It puts a damper on the prom even before it begins.

WISDOM: *When faced with situations that are unpredictable or inconvenient, look at them as opportunities to refine the inner qualities of your heart and mind and develop equanimity. Thrive in the situation and remain balanced while abandoning judgments and opinions.*

SITUATION: While on a date, you wave at someone you think you know. You tell your date that you haven't seen this person in a while and want to catch up to them. Still waving, you hustle to catch up. Then you realize that it is not the person you thought it was.

WISDOM: *Transcend your predicaments with laughter.*

SITUATION: You accidentally walk in on your roommate having sex with her boyfriend. Before you realize what's happening, you see them in a kinky position. You feel really weird every time you look at your roommate and her boyfriend now.

WISDOM: *When you are overwhelmed by people and what they are doing and you need to lighten up, remember, everyone is a little crazy in their own way.*

SITUATION: An ex-boyfriend told a mutual friend a secret about something you did in the past that you told him about in confidence. You never wanted anyone else to find out about this.

WISDOM: *It does not matter what anyone else says about you because you cannot control what anyone else says. The only thing you can control is your reaction to what is said.*

SITUATION: The boy you have been dating for a long time wants to take the relationship to the next level, but you are not ready, so he threatens to break up with you. You've been through a lot of changes and challenges recently, and you feel hurt by the threat of abandonment.

WISDOM: *If you have an awareness of your feelings as feelings, it becomes possible to break out of the passive or hostile modes that you automatically fall into when feeling threatened by abandonment.*

SITUATION: In a moment of lust and pursuit of pleasure, you contracted a sexually transmitted disease. While the STD is treatable, the pain, suffering, and guilt are leaving a mark on you.

WISDOM: *Most of the pain and suffering we experience in our pursuit of pleasure is caused by ourselves. We mistake pleasure for happiness even though we know pleasure doesn't make us happy. Pleasure is pleasure, a temporary gratification of desire. Happiness is a deeper satisfaction, a feeling of wholeness, of non-neediness, of being mindful of life.*

SITUATION: Your best friend likes someone and wants to go out with him. But the person she wants to go out with asks you out instead. You say "no" and explain that your friend likes him. Unfortunately, he said that he's not interested in her. You know that your friend is going to find out what happened, and you do not know how to tell her without hurting her.

WISDOM: *Speaking honestly needs to be linked to a heart of kindness and compassion. The vast majority of problems in relationships come from communications that lack honesty, empathy, or love.*

SITUATION: Someone asks you out on a date, and you politely decline, but you have noticed that he now appears to be stalking you. You do not feel physically threatened and do not want to make a big deal out of it, but you are a little concerned because you see these scenarios on television and in the news all the time.

WISDOM: *Generally, if you worry about your situation, you complicate it, adding mental suffering.*

SITUATION: It has been tough getting back the romance in your life after a nasty breakup. You just found out someone has a crush on you, and you think you can have romantic feelings toward that person. But, you are afraid to get hurt again.

WISDOM: *Happiness and love come naturally in letting go of fear.*

SITUATION: For a very long time you have liked someone who is a friend as more than just a friend. You never thought you were in his league, so you never proceeded to act on your feelings. But lately you feel very good about yourself, and you're going to take a chance and let this person know that you are interested in them as more than just a friend.

WISDOM: *When you realize that you are complete, and always have been, new freedom and happiness will come to you.*

SITUATION: Someone you know likes you in a romantic way, and while you are flattered by the interest, you would prefer to simply enjoy this person's company as a friend and not move beyond that. You have heard that he is going to ask you out on a date, and you don't know how you can turn him down and still remain friends.

WISDOM: *Being honest does not mean being hurtful. Being mindful does not always mean being nice. If you are honest and mindful, you will act from kindness of heart.*

SITUATION: After a long relationship with a boyfriend, you realize that you don't love him anymore. You like him very much and want him to be happy in life, but you also have to be honest with yourself. He is a nice guy who's good looking, and all your friends like him, but you feel that breaking up is the right thing to do so you can move on.

WISDOM: *There is very little time to life, so it is important that you spend each second being fully awake, more compassionate, more loving, more caring, more honest, more mindful, and really living your life. Every day is truly an opportunity for you.*

SITUATION: Your heart was broken by someone you still love. No matter how hard you try to suppress your love and move on, you just can't. You know there is no chance for the relationship to resume, but you just don't know how to cope with your broken heart.

WISDOM: *While pain and times of change can cause discomfort and bring out our deepest fears, they can also be an invitation to new encounters and hope. Pain often nudges us to grow.*

SITUATION: You are dating someone you like a lot but do not love. The relationship is too new for you to know whether you may be able to love him. It has not gone past the kissing stage, and that's just where you want it to stay for now. But he wants the relationship to take the next step and is pressuring you to have sex.

WISDOM: *Compatibility cannot be forced. A successful relationship is based on truth, so be true to yourself. You can only control your own actions. Succumbing to a sexual relationship when you are not ready is a shallow substitute for fulfillment.*

SITUATION: Since your divorce, you've been surprised at how tricky the dating scene seems to be. There seems to be a lot more game playing and untruthfulness than you remember. You do not like to play such games, and you try to be as truthful as you can.

WISDOM: *Let the entire game happen on its own without changing or manipulating anything.*

SITUATION: When you were younger, you were a bit of a free spirit—and sexually promiscuous. Those days are gone, and you are much more mature now, but it is difficult for you to free yourself from the past, and you dwell on the mistakes that you made.

WISDOM: *By living in the present moment with all your powers, you are doing everything you can to free yourself from the past.*

SITUATION: You recently divorced after 25 years of marriage and now you are trying to get back into the dating scene. There is someone you would like to ask out on a date, but you realize that the rules have changed dramatically since you were younger, and you really don't know how to go about dating anymore.

WISDOM: *A person with inward courage dares to live.*

SITUATION: During an argument, your boyfriend says that you are very predictable and don't have a creative bone in your body. This hurts you, though you have to admit that there is some truth to it. You have become a little predictable lately.

WISDOM: *Look at everything as though it is the first time you are looking at it. Look at life like a child would. See the magic in life. Don't be afraid to put in the effort to achieve this.*

SITUATION: You were in a relationship with someone that ended on a bad note. At one time the relationship was filled with love. After you've had to time to get over the hurt, you move on with your life. Unfortunately, the same cannot be said about the other person. He has let it be known through mutual friends that he just does not like you.

WISDOM: *The only way to defeat hate is through love. Love takes the energy out of hate through compassion. Love truly does conquer all.*

SITUATION: On a date, you got caught up in the moment and lied about your position at your workplace. You didn't know you would have more than one date with this person, so you didn't really care about your boasting. Now you realize you like this person and would like to date him again, but you are caught up in a lie that will eventually unravel if the relationship continues.

WISDOM: *Abstain from all forms of lying. Whether outright lying, exaggerating, or minimizing, a lie will always be a lie. Speaking should be truthful, useful, and appropriate while causing no harm. Lies are habit forming and they take you away from your goals of spiritual practice.*

SITUATION: When you were young, you were in love with someone who did not think a career was important. He was more concerned about making the world a better place and having fun than about making a lot of money. Some of the best times of your life were spent with him. But you were into your career and were making big bucks and wanted to meet a person who had the same goals, so you broke up with him. Then you found yourself in a series of shallow relationships. To this day, you think breaking up with him was your single biggest mistake.

WISDOM: *Everyone makes errors of judgment throughout their lives. Don't beat yourself up over them. Forgive yourself. Look at mistakes as lessons and chances to make lucky discoveries along your journey.*

SITUATION: At your 25th high school reunion, you run into an old boyfriend. You remember him very well. Your special relationship lasted junior and senior years in high school and freshman year in college. When you two broke up, your heart was broken. You are surprised at how well he looks. Even more surprising, your heart races when you see him. You both have happy marriages and wonderful children, but you can't help thinking he might be the one who got away.

WISDOM: *See the events in your life without distortions so that you can mindfully let go of your stories and dispel the doubt they generate.*

SITUATION: You cannot even explain the incident to yourself, let alone someone else. After a few alcoholic drinks, you got caught up in the moment and let your guard down. The one-night stand with a stranger did not feel like an adventure, the way it is often portrayed in movies. You are in uncharted territory. You are not only consumed with guilt but also worried about having contracted some type of STD.

WISDOM: *Aware of the suffering caused by sexual misconduct, commit to cultivating responsibility and learning ways to protect the safety and integrity of individuals, couples, family, and society. Resolve not to engage in sexual relations without love and a long-term commitment.*

SITUATION: Planning your wedding is overwhelming. You did not realize that it was going to be so time-consuming. The pressure of the event is distracting your mind and filling it with doubts.

WISDOM: *Learn to live fully in the moment, not lost in dreams, plans, memories, or the commentaries of the thinking mind. There is a big difference between drinking a cup of tea while being there completely and drinking a cup of tea while thinking about five other things. It is only by being fully in the moment that the fundamental questions of the heart can be answered. Simplify and take each step one at a time.*

SITUATION: As you enter your thirties, you are finding it more difficult to date. The old saying that "all the good ones have been taken" seems to be true. Family and friends are pressuring you to find a man and settle down, and you are beginning to worry about the whole thing. While you want to have a family with the right person, you know that you have not met him yet.

WISDOM: *Many people think that if only they were in a relationship with someone, they would be happy, but that is doubtful. Relationships need to happen naturally, they cannot be forced. Get as much happiness out of what you are doing as you can, and don't put off being happy until some future date.*

SITUATION: You plan to propose to your girlfriend at a tailgate at a football game. It's raining so hard that you decide to have a picnic in the living room instead and watch the game on television. It becomes that much more memorable.

WISDOM: *Whatever the day's weather, you must accept it. To complain about the rain, or lack of it, shows a mind out of tune with nature.*

SITUATION: Your boyfriend pops the question, asking for your hand in marriage. While you know you love him, you are not sure you're ready for marriage yet.

WISDOM: *Move slowly and maintain a depth of commitment that can be sustained over the long haul.*

SITUATION: Having met the person of your dreams, you are beginning to think about life differently. As your relationship develops, talk of children keeps coming up. You are skeptical about having children because you are insecure about whether you would be a good parent. You did not have good parental role models, and your childhood was dysfunctional and unhappy. You just don't know if you have the skills to be a good parent.

WISDOM: *Happy people are good parents.*

Marriage

SITUATION: You are getting married soon. You want your relationship with your spouse to grow over the years. You want to form a bond with your spouse that gets deeper with time. You do not want to end up like couples you know who are unhappy with each other and do not enjoy each others' company.

WISDOM: *According to the Buddha's teachings, the most basic condition for happiness is freedom from anger, despair, jealousy, and delusion.*

SITUATION: Your spouse usually vacuums the house because it is the one job you cannot stand doing. Unfortunately, right now he is injured and can't do the vacuuming for a while.

WISDOM: *What you do, really do it—without dreading it or resenting it.*

SITUATION: You cannot believe what a stupid thing you did to your spouse. You cannot feel bad enough for what you did.

WISDOM: *Forgive yourself when your old habits get in your way. When you smile a smile of compassion, you encourage your loving kindness to wake up. You encourage yourself to be kind to yourself because you are a thinking being.*

SITUATION: Your spouse lied to you about something important. Although there was an apology, you feel the matter has not been completely resolved.

WISDOM: *If you practice nonaggression when you feel irritated with your spouse, instead of aggravating the situation with anger, you can resolve your differences peacefully and maintain harmony.*

SITUATION: The distribution of parenting in your household is not equal. You both have careers and busy lives, yet you give much more of your time and energy to child-rearing than your spouse does.

WISDOM: *When you are practicing generosity, you have to give up things that you might enjoy. You realize the benefits that come from saying no to your greed and allowing others to enjoy what you're giving away.*

SITUATION: You have trouble letting your spouse go out with his friends. You trust him and recognize that it is healthy to go out with friends, but you still have trouble letting him go.

WISDOM: *Can you stop clinging to others, trying to shape and control them, and instead allow them more space, freedom, and time? From possessiveness comes conflict; letting go gives satisfaction.*

SITUATION: After many years of marriage, it is very evident that you and your spouse have developed different goals. You are still trying to climb the corporate ladder, and he is content where he is in his job. You are trying to convince him to change and become more aggressive about his career advancement.

WISDOM: *You're trying to change the wrong person. If you want people to do more, praise them and appreciate what they are already doing.*

SITUATION: You feel bad because you have learned that your spouse makes excuses and rationalizes your troublesome behavior to family members and friends.

WISDOM: *There is a way to erase some of our negative karma: purification. It requires understanding that you have behaved badly in the past and taking full responsibility for this behavior. Then you must sincerely regret and repent your negative actions and promise yourself to try not to behave badly again. Try to perform only positive, virtuous actions from now on.*

SITUATION: You make about half the household's money and still do around three-quarters of the housecleaning and child-rearing.

WISDOM: *Don't attach to the idea that life is fair.*

SITUATION: You and your spouse are at an impasse about college choices for your child. The two options are a large state school, at a reasonable cost, and a small, expensive private school. The cost of the school is a significant factor in your consideration. Each of you has strong feelings about which school is best suited for your child.

WISDOM: *When you are grounded in calmness and moment-to-moment awareness, you are more likely to be creative and see new options and new solutions to problems. You become aware of emotions and less carried away by them, and you can maintain your balance and perspective in trying circumstances.*

SITUATION: Everything is going very nicely on an evening out with your husband until you say something you know will start a fight and ruin the night. You were having a good time, and now you don't even know why you said what you did.

WISDOM: *Speech is based on thoughts. If we learn to control our thoughts, we have control over our speech.*

SITUATION: You find asking for help difficult because you feel that it is a sign of weakness. But you are having major marital problems and feel that you do need to seek guidance.

WISDOM: *After you ask for guidance—listen!*

SITUATION: You run into an old boyfriend coming home from work. You stop to have a drink with him and catch up on things. It's really just an innocent get-together. Later, when you arrive home, your husband asks where you have been. You consider telling him you were tied up in traffic.

WISDOM: *People are most vulnerable when they are lying, and it is usually more difficult than telling the truth.*

SITUATION: Your spouse regularly listens to a TV and radio personality who believes that he know everything and is not afraid to tell his listeners so. Sometimes you get the feeling that your spouse really believes what this guy is saying.

WISDOM: *Anyone who thinks that they know and understand what is really going on, probably does not.*

SITUATION: For the past 20 years, you and your wife have been exchanging cards on the anniversary of the day you met. It has become a special ritual. Over the past few months, you have been busy with work and feeling stressed. Unfortunately, you forgot to get her a card this year, and she feels sad and hurt about it.

WISDOM: *Forgetfulness is the opposite of mindfulness. You drink a cup of tea, but you do not know you are drinking a cup of tea. You sit with the person you love, but you don't know she is there. You walk, but you are not really walking. You are someplace else, thinking about the past or the future, your career or the economy. The horse of your habit energy carries you along like a captive. Stop the horse and reclaim your freedom.*

SITUATION: You are trying to remember your spouse's cell phone number, but for some reason it is eluding you.

WISDOM: *The mind is like a puppy, wandering endlessly and delighting in each new distraction. An antidote to forgetfulness and distraction is concentration. Take a moment and count breaths to 10, then start again.*

SITUATION: You are so angry with your spouse for saying something hurtful to you that you cannot even think rationally. Angry words just spew from your mouth. You feel like you have no control over the words or the anger behind them.

WISDOM: *Before your anger does injury to another, it is done to yourself. Anger is like picking up hot coals with your bare hands and trying to throw them at the person you're angry at. Who gets burned first? The one who is angry, of course. Overcoming anger leads to peace of mind without regrets.*

SITUATION: To make your love life a little more exciting, you and your spouse begin to look at pornographic sites on the Internet. After viewing some of them, you feel guilty and sad instead of excited.

WISDOM: *Pornography can create a hostile and unsafe environment for men and women as well as an unrealistic and unhealthy view of sexuality. Some forms of pornography go against the third Buddhist precept—to refrain from sexual misconduct—and should be avoided.*

SITUATION: You've been around your spouse for a long time, and you know he's a very bright person. But it does bother you that his spelling and grammar skills are poor.

WISDOM: *Cease watching for faults in others. Instead, be aware and ready to judge whether your own deeds are correct or incorrect. When you judge others, you are the one who feels pain. Learn to see what's not important and realize that everyone is doing the best they possibly can.*

SITUATION: No matter how many times you tell your husband to put the toilet seat back down, he does not listen. You just don't get it. It makes you angry because it is just a matter of his listening.

WISDOM: *Anger not only negatively affects your mind but also damages you physically by increasing your heart rate and elevating your blood pressure. Compassion looks into the other person—the listener—and feels whether the time is right for that person to hear your truth.*

SITUATION: It seems like you never get the credit you deserve from people. When you were young, your parents never acknowledged your good grades. Now your spouse does not seem to recognize the hard work and good deeds you do.

WISDOM: *Thoughts have a way of amplifying external difficulties, ideas of inadequacy and loneliness, and feelings of rejection, leading you deeper into delusion. By choosing to transform your mind, you can weaken this delusion and not be enslaved by your thoughts. It is your choice.*

SITUATION: You love your husband, but you feel frustrated because he does not do his fair share of responsibilities around the house. You just don't get it. You work a full-time job just like him, but you still have to do more the household chores and child-rearing. He seems to need so much downtime to recover from life, and it's driving you crazy.

WISDOM: *Feeling strong emotions is a part of life, and there is nothing wrong with them when you learn to relate to them skillfully instead of becoming obsessed with them. When strong emotions arise in your life, find refuge and stabilize yourself through your breath. By going to your breath, you can feel the calmness that breathing deeply provides.*

SITUATION: Your spouse is driving you nuts. He never seems to be able to remember anything. Even when you write things down for him, he does not remember them. He seems to be going in a thousand directions at once. You do not believe a medical condition is causing this. Between work and family responsibilities, he seems to be overwhelmed. You sympathize with him, but you need him to be better about remembering things.

WISDOM: *When the mind is scattered and not calm, a person does not have serenity. When a person does not have serenity, he cannot concentrate and loses all of his energy to distraction.*

SITUATION: Although you love your husband and appreciate all he has done for you, it is difficult for you to accept his lack of career motivation. He seems to be content with his job and has no interest in moving up the ladder.

WISDOM: *To love someone is to be happy with who and what they are, accepting them without conditions. If your heart can become loving and accepting, if you can harbor no anger or resentment, then you have taken a great step on the dharma path.*

SITUATION: You feel that the time is right for you to begin having a family, but your spouse refuses to discuss the matter with you. Every time you try to bring it up, either she ignores you or you get into a fight. You are beginning to punish her with your words and actions because you are frustrated by her silence on the issue.

WISDOM: *Whenever you are about to do or say something, ask yourself if the action or words will result in well-being or harm to yourself or to others. If well-being, then do or say it. If harm, then do not do or say it.*

SITUATION: You are so angry with yourself because of what you said to your spouse. He was recently passed over for a job promotion. When he told you the disappointing news, you blamed him for not getting the promotion. You spoke out of frustration and really did not mean what you said.

WISDOM: *Calm the mind by creating a mind state where there is no self-hatred because of your actions, speech, thoughts, fears, or desires. Your state of mind will become gentle and spacious enough to see things as they truly are.*

SITUATION: After you and your spouse lost a baby due to miscarriage, you've noticed that your spouse has become quick to start fights with you over both large and small things. You realize that she is in pain over the loss of the baby, and you are trying to defuse the fights as best you can.

WISDOM: *Love alone is the only thing big enough to hold all the pain of this world.*

SITUATION: Your husband has the annoying habit of checking his stock portfolio frequently. Now that he can access the Internet with a hand-held device, the habit is much worse. You can understand checking it when the stock market is open, but you don't get why he checks it when the stock market is closed.

WISDOM: *Can you see the Buddha in others, even when they annoy you?*

SITUATION: When you fell in love with your spouse, you thought your life would change and all your problems would be solved. The love is still there after an exhausting few years, but so are your problems.

WISDOM: *Relationships cannot be entered into with the notion that they are an antidote to your problems or that the other person is going to be responsible for having a positive change on your life. While relationships may help you grow as an individual, they will not solve your problems.*

SITUATION: You and your spouse argue not over money or how to raise the kids but about the temperature in the house. You are always too hot and he is always too cold. Whenever either of you passes the thermostat, you change the temperature, thus making the other person uncomfortable and renewing the argument.

WISDOM: *As long as you retain the notion of self, you'll feel uncomfortable, rigid, and grasping, and people will find your egotistical self unpleasant. You'll get upset or angry when someone disagrees with you or blames you for something, when things disappoint you or don't go your way, and even when somebody offers you constructive criticism.*

SITUATION: You did not see this one coming—the classic case of the older businessman falling for the younger secretary. Your husband of 30 years is asking for a divorce because, he says, he has fallen in love at work. You feel as if you are outside your body, you are so hurt and betrayed. You just do not understand how or why he is doing this to you after so many years of a marriage that, though maybe not perfect, has been filled with respect, love, and resolve until death do you part.

WISDOM: *Abandon thoughts of blame and hate. Live in love.*

SITUATION: When you and your spouse go out for a dinner date and leave the children with a babysitter, you check your cell phone obsessively to see if the sitter or kids have called. You know this behavior has a negative impact on your spouse and negates the purpose of going out and enjoying yourself, but you can't seem to stop yourself.

WISDOM: *A person can make any number of irrational defenses to justify obsessive-compulsive behavior, which comes from fear of surrendering control and giving up security—which you never really have to begin with. Expose yourself to your fears in appropriate steps and measures to diminish their power over you. Teach yourself to be in the present moment so you can respond appropriately to whatever unexpected or unpleasant demands life throws at you.*

SITUATION: You and your spouse have talked about how you want to raise your children when you decide to have them. You want to make sure that you're both on the same page about what is important for children to cultivate and develop as they grow. You don't want such issues to cause confrontations later.

WISDOM: *Children can cultivate fundamental human virtues when they develop a good heart, stability and reliability, and an ease with themselves that lets them be at ease with others.*

SITUATION: Your spouse is going through a personal crisis that you cannot figure out. You are trying so hard to do everything that you can to make her happy, but it is not working. It seems like the harder you try, the less happy she becomes.

WISDOM: *Effort may be counterproductive to happiness. Instead of producing happiness, trying too hard may do just the opposite. Relax in the present moment and don't demand that things get better. Let things work themselves out and happiness will be found.*

SITUATION: Your spouse's 50th birthday is approaching. She requests that nothing special be done for her birthday; she wants to celebrate it quietly. But you go ahead and arrange a surprise party.

WISDOM: *Have the humility to mindfully and accurately assess your intentions and motivations, your strengths and weaknesses, so that you may recognize your spiritual interrelatedness with other beings and respect their own intentions and motivations.*

SITUATION: Whenever your spouse overeats, he snores and periodically wakes you up during the night, disrupting your sleep pattern and making for a tough next day. You know that he does not do this to hurt you, but it is negatively affecting you.

WISDOM: *Be at peace and your suffering will end.*

SITUATION: Dinner conversations between you and your spouse have changed dramatically since your children left for college. No longer are the children your main topic of conversation. It feels a little weird because for 20 years, mealtime conversation somehow always managed to turn into a discussion about the children.

WISDOM: *One things leads to another. Just as a flame can be passed from one candle to another on a birthday cake, your compassion and enthusiasm can be passed on to all you touch. Infuse your conversations with passion for whatever you are into now.*

SITUATION: Your husband is going through what appears to be a long-term midlife crisis. He is having a difficult time adjusting to the emotional and hormonal changes that happen at his age. This has been going on for a while, and you are worried not only about him, but also about how his behavior and actions are affecting you.

WISDOM: *Nurturing calmness, understanding, and trust within yourself directly impacts your way of seeing each person and encounter that enters your life.*

SITUATION: It is retirement time. After many years of planning, you and your spouse are packing up and moving to a different state. Now that it is finally happening, you are feeling scared about the change.

WISDOM: *Freedom and happiness are found in flexibility and the ability to deal with change easily.*

SITUATION: After being married for 30 years, you still wonder if your spouse really knows you. For that matter, can a person really know another person?

WISDOM: *You are a combination of your genetic heritage, your life history, and the social conditions in which you have lived. You come into the world innocent and pure, carrying both genetics and the karma you created in previous lives. During your present lifetime, your human nature is changed by what you are taught and what you have learned. Despite this, you can always return to your Buddha nature, your goodness, and your capacity for mindfulness, calm, and seeing deeply.*

SITUATION: After being happily married—at least so you thought—for a long time, your spouse leaves you for another person. The pain is truly overwhelming.

WISDOM: *Meditate on forgiveness for those who have hurt or harmed you: "There are many ways I have been wounded and hurt, abused, and abandoned by others in thought, word, or deed, knowingly or unknowingly. In the many ways others have hurt or harmed me, out of fear, pain, confusion, or anger, I see these now. To the extent I am ready, I offer them forgiveness. I have carried this pain in my heart too long. For this reason, to those who have caused me harm, I offer you my forgiveness."*

SITUATION: After your divorce, the pain and self-hatred is real and strong. Your spouse left you for a younger person, and now you feel that there is something wrong with you.

WISDOM: *If you cannot find tranquility, peace, and love within yourself, it will be difficult to find it elsewhere. A profound daily practice can be to whittle away your self-hatred with loving kindness.*

Parents and Kids

SITUATION: You are not ready to be pregnant yet. You still feel you have so much more to do before you start a family. But you find yourself in a situation you never thought you would be in: pregnant and unmarried.

WISDOM: *A balanced attitude can afford you true happiness. Equanimity is one of the highest kinds of happiness. When events change from good to bad, pleasant to painful, or easy to difficult, remain balanced and undisturbed. Embrace the extremes without getting thrown off balance, and take everything in stride.*

SITUATION: It has taken you a long time to get pregnant. You'd almost given up. You are very happy right now.

WISDOM: *When you are happy, meditate for a few moments and be grateful for that feeling.*

SITUATION: After a long and difficult pregnancy, you give birth to a beautiful, healthy child. You are happy that everything has turned out okay, but you are now worried about the future and what life has in store for your child.

WISDOM: *Enjoy and appreciate what is before your eyes. Shake off all worries and anxieties. Don't think of the future; don't think of the past. Just enjoy the present moment.*

SITUATION: After having your baby, you are experiencing a case of the "baby blues." The baby and you are physically healthy. It is just that, emotionally, you are a bit down. You try to talk to your husband about it, but he does not understand. He is busy with his work and the new responsibility of a child. Emotionally, he is doing better than you.

WISDOM: *If happiness comes, don't become too excited. If sorrow comes, don't become too depressed. Happiness and sorrow are not you. Watch, unattached. Happiness and suffering depend upon your own mind, upon your interpretation. They do not come from others.*

SITUATION: After difficulty conceiving a child, the odds of getting pregnant with another child are slim. You and your spouse are thinking of going the foster care route to complete your family, but two problems have arisen. First, family members and friends are trying to talk you out of it. Second, you have fallen in love with two brothers in the foster care unit. You can't imagine separating them, but you only want one more child.

WISDOM: *No matter how messed-up you feel, you all have goodness at your core. Once you have seen how much better it is to do good than to do evil, you will begin to have even greater trust in your own inherent goodness. Meditation and good intentions can generate a powerful inner voice that will keep you on track.*

SITUATION: At school, your child has been studying the environment and the negative effect humans have on it. Your child wants to start a compost pile to help eliminate excess garbage. You know it means more work for you, but setting a good example is important.

WISDOM: *We produce garbage every day, so we need to practice continually taking care of our garbage so as to make it into flowers.*

SITUATION: When you are out, your spouse lets the children stay up past their bedtime to finish playing a game. When you come home and see that they are still awake, you become angry at your spouse and the kids.

WISDOM: *You wonder how you can uproot the confusion that starts an argument. Just acknowledge the state of mind, as if in meditation, by naming it and giving it space. Shine the light of awareness on it, and it loses its power over you.*

SITUATION: It is the weekend again. The kids have that "What do we do now?" look on their faces.

WISDOM: *Go on a Saturday picnic instead of shopping at a mall.*

SITUATION: You wonder if kids still enjoy jumping into a leaf pile. Come to think of it, you wonder if *you* still enjoy jumping into a leaf pile.

WISDOM: *Rake leaves and jump in the pile.*

SITUATION: You and your spouse want to sell your house and move to a different state. But you promised your child that you would stay in your present community until he is done with high school in two years.

WISDOM: *True patience manifests itself as a non-grasping openness to whatever comes next. It is a calm willingness to be present.*

SITUATION: Teaching your child to hit a tennis ball with her racquet is more challenging than you expected because of her lack of concentration.

WISDOM: *Use meditation to teach concentration. Right concentration means working on achieving a one-pointed mind. If you are doing something, concentrate wholly on what you are doing.*

SITUATION: After watching your child interact with other children at the park, you realize that he seems to switch from activity to activity and person to person very rapidly without really focusing.

WISDOM: *The master directs his straying thoughts. By ruling them, he finds happiness.*

SITUATION: You catch yourself yelling at your child again for doing something thoughtless. Parenting is a difficult job, and you are vowing to become a better parent.

WISDOM: *In meditation, when you put distance between yourself and your thoughts, your mind becomes relaxed, flexible, workable, pliable, and you have more clarity about your direction in life.*

SITUATION: It seems like your spouse and children are ganging up on you. Whenever you make a suggestion, plan a meal, or organize a family event, the entire group criticizes you and nixes the idea.

WISDOM: *If you catch yourself being paranoid or taking things personally, question the logic of it. Is somebody really trying to annoy or hurt you? Are they simply going about their business or being oblivious or ignorant toward you? Irritations and annoyances can be unpleasant, but you do not need to take them personally or react to them.*

SITUATION: The dreaded snow day from school has occurred. As a telecommuter, you are busy with a lot of work at home. Your child is behaving very poorly, and it's not helping.

WISDOM: *When your child is not behaving to your liking, you can easily become irritated. If your understanding and compassion are not strong enough to protect you, you will allow that person's behavior to provoke the seed of irritation within you. With a compassionate state of mind, your actions will always carry a tone of kindness and softness that is useful in overcoming a child's problem behavior.*

SITUATION: When you signed up for having children, you knew it was not going to be an easy job, especially when they became teenagers. You were prepared for certain things, having been a teenager yourself. But dealing with disrespectfulness is taking just about everything out of you.

WISDOM: *Children are to be embraced and treasured for the difficulty they bring.*

SITUATION: Your child's friend's parents are overly permissive. They seem to never say "no," letting the kids have the run of the house. Every time your child goes over to their house, he comes back with another story about what they are allowed to do there.

WISDOM: *You do all those things for which you criticize people you don't like in your life, all those people you judge. Try to just look at what you do and how you handle things, and don't worry about what others do.*

SITUATION: You knew it was going to happen, but no book can prepare you for your child going through puberty. You realize that he is going through major physical and mental changes, but you are being impacted, too. You don't know how you are going to survive this.

WISDOM: *Stay aware of the flow, of the fact that everything is in ceaseless change. If you remain open to experience and change, you will find yourself able to deal with life's different weathers.*

SITUATION: Your son has been begging you to play Monopoly for weeks. You have been putting it off for one reason or another because you just cannot stand playing board games. Finally, you give in and set up a family night of Monopoly.

WISDOM: *When you are happily present in the present moment, you are present for your spouse, children, relatives, and friends.*

SITUATION: As a parent, you only want what is best for your child. After years of chauffeuring her around to soccer games, she informs you that she does not want to try out for the high school soccer team. She is no longer happy playing soccer and wants to try a different sport. Your expectations are shattered. She was one of the best players on the team.

WISDOM: *Who is making you angry? Perhaps the anger is subtly directed at you. When your expectations are not met, you tend to blame others and become angry. Expectations get in the way and distort the picture.*

SITUATION: Your child comes home from school very upset because some of the other kids called him a nerd and a geek during science class.

WISDOM: *When someone insults you, be intelligent enough to see that the other person suffers from his own words and anger. Do not retaliate by returning the sarcasm or slander, but practice patience instead. An insult becomes yours only if you choose to accept and engage it. An insult can only come from within, not from a situation.*

SITUATION: You have been collecting Hummel figurines since you were young. One day your son is roughhousing with the dog, and they bump into the cabinet where the Hummels are displayed, breaking a few of them. You can't recount the number of times you told him not to play by this cabinet. The blood rushes to your head, and you explode with anger. Your son tries to apologize, but your anger is too intense to even hear it.

WISDOM: *Although you may still be irritated, you will not lose yourself to anger. Be patient with the harm. Forbear from reacting. Let go, accept, and forgive.*

SITUATION: Your unwed teenage daughter gives you news that all parents of teenage daughters dread: she is pregnant.

WISDOM: *There will always be troubles, suffering, and pain in this world. Trying to escape it is not the answer. Opening your heart and mind and trying to help is an answer.*

SITUATION: You will be the first to admit that you do not read many books. After a long day at work and dealing with family things, the last thing you want to do is to read. You would rather sit in front of the television and veg out. But now your children are reaching the reading age, and you want to set a good example for them.

WISDOM: *Read slowly and calmly, with your mind cut off from all thinking so that the very act of reading is peace. Take a break every 15 minutes and close your eyes for a minute to help bring your attention back to breath. Enjoy the words on the pages.*

SITUATION: No matter how hard you try, you find yourself yelling at your spouse and children time and time again. You want to discover why you keep repeating this pattern.

WISDOM: *Everyone has personal difficulties that they tend to run into over and over again.*

SITUATION: The event calendar on your refrigerator is filled up. Trying to coordinate the comings and goings of everyone in the family is challenging. You just do not have the time to attend or take children to all the events that are coming up.

WISDOM: *Daily life usually does not offer the kind of time needed for reflection. Yet reflective time provides a chance to focus inward and listen to the wise voice within. By turning inside to connect with your natural wisdom, clarity ensues, and problems may be solved effortlessly and effectively.*

SITUATION: It worries you that, because your children are more computer literate than you are, it is hard for you to keep track of the websites they visit. You just do not know which sites are trustworthy and which ones take advantage of your children.

WISDOM: *Take precautions, but meet this transient world with neither grasping nor fear. Trust the unfolding of life, and you will attain true serenity.*

SITUATION: Halloween is great fun. You fondly remember taking the kids out trick-or-treating. Now, your high school–aged child informs you that he is going trick-or-treating with some friends. You feel that this is not in the spirit of Halloween—they're too old to trick-or-treat.

WISDOM: *Be a good human being, a warm-hearted affectionate person. Having a sense of caring, a feeling of compassion, will bring you happiness and peace of mind and automatically create a positive atmosphere.*

SITUATION: Your 12-year-old daughter matured young and looks and acts older than her age. This has led to a host of problems for you. She has been asked out on a date by a 14-year-old boy from her school. Although you know the boy and his family, you don't know whether you are comfortable with your daughter going on a date. You realize things have changed since you were young, but you feel she is still too young. On the flip side, you want to avoid starting a big fight and coming across as a fuddy-duddy.

WISDOM: *If you recognize worry for what it is, acknowledge it, put it in perspective, and refuse to let it control you—that's cultivating Zen living.*

SITUATION: You only allow your children one half-hour of television during the school week, but you do make exceptions for educational programs. You do believe there is some value in these types of shows.

WISDOM: *Watching television hardly ever promotes physiological or psychological relaxation. You can teach mindful consumption of television.*

SITUATION: Your daughter performs chores around the house and gets a small allowance for her work. She asks if she can have a raise in her allowance. When you ask why, she says that a couple of her friends make five times the amount she does for similar chores.

WISDOM: *Choose your fights wisely. If there is a way to compromise here, do so. You can try to convey the message, though, to accept what you are given and never be envious.*

SITUATION: Your son has been diagnosed with attention deficit disorder. You really do not want to start him on medication, but you also do not want him to fall behind in school. You are concerned about the side effects from the medication.

WISDOM: *Act on an intuitive feeling. Act on what is right in your own heart, and there will be victory.*

SITUATION: This week is Turn Off the TV week at your son's school. He is making a pledge to not watch television for the entire week. He is getting the whole family involved by having everyone in the family make the same pledge. You think it might feel good to go on an information diet for a week. You may even extend it to newspapers and magazines.

WISDOM: *Constantly devote yourself to the cleansing of your own mind.*

SITUATION: Talk about spoiling your children! During the holiday season, purchases went way beyond being sane. Between what they got from you and what they got from the grandparents, your children received so many presents it just does not feel right. The spirit of the holiday seems to be lost, and the only thing that matters is the number of presents they receive. It seems wasteful and like a poor lesson for your children to learn.

WISDOM: *Ask the grandparents to join you in a concerted effort to raise your children in a spiritual way that will benefit the planet. Earth should be a better place because they are here.*

SITUATION: Parental responsibility is taking a dramatic toll on your freedom. You can no longer do many of things you used to enjoy because of all the responsibilities that come with having children. You miss some of your past freedom.

WISDOM: *The purpose of a spiritual life and the secret to happiness is to understand that freedom is possible. No matter how busy you are or what is going on in your life, you can discover freedom, not in wanting, having, keeping, or holding on to things, but in the natural goodness of your heart.*

SITUATION: Your son wants a popular new video-game player. You feel that such devices are addictive and harmful to children, and you will not let him own one. It is causing tension in your family. Your son cannot understand why you will not let him get one, even with his own money. He says all his friends have them.

WISDOM: *Opening your heart and mind, fully hear what your son and others tell you so that you may nourish understanding and strengthen the connection between you.*

SITUATION: You let your child push you over the edge, and out of anger and frustration, you spanked him. It is the first time that you have ever laid a physical hand on him. You felt the anger and frustration come out as you spanked him on his bottom. Afterward, you felt guilty about the incident.

WISDOM: *You need not have committed a crime to feel guilt. An everyday incident can cause remorse. Guilt is a negative emotion unless you use it as motivation to learn, change, and act more responsibly. Mindfully let go of guilt. Draw on experiences to shape a present that will cause no guilt in the future.*

SITUATION: One of your children is a natural optimist, and the other is a natural pessimist. Their personalities are so polarized that you find it difficult to manage them and plan things.

WISDOM: *Everyone wants to be happy—the optimists and the pessimists. Teach children to cultivate gratitude, generosity, and kindness. Teach them by your own example to be fully present for the many blessings in your life. You will show them how one gains happiness through gratitude for even the smallest wonders.*

SITUATION: When work gets crazy, the first thing to go is family time. You feel bad about neglecting them, but your salary pays for all the nice things that you have. If you only had an extra hour a day, you could get back your family time.

WISDOM: *When you are around family, be completely present. The greatest gift you can offer anyone is your true presence.*

SITUATION: In talking with your teenager, you would like to talk on their level and not overstep their boundaries.

WISDOM: *For a teen, be present—even in silence—ready to listen without judgment and with an open mind.*

SITUATION: Your teenage daughter has been driving for over a year without any major incidents. She gets good grades, behaves well, and is learning to be more independent. You get into an argument with her because after she gets out of school, she wants to drive to a friend's house and sleep over. You want to keep her safe and feel that she should bring the car home. Then you can take her to the friend's house.

WISDOM: *Do a brief meditation for cultivating compassion when you are having difficulty with a loved one or friend. Sit, looking beyond the conflict, and reflect on the fact that this person is a human being like you. This person has the same desire for happiness and well-being, the same fear of suffering, the same need for love. Note how this meditation softens your feelings.*

SITUATION: You catch your teenage child and some of his friends with alcohol.

WISDOM: *There is no teacher like one's own experience.*

SITUATION: It is midnight, and your teenager is not home yet. He is a half-hour late and is not answering his cell phone. You are not sure what to do next.

WISDOM: *Try to see difficult circumstances and happenings as bad-tasting medicine, or as learning experiences. Look at the reality of the situation without resistance, struggle, aversion, or avoidance. Breathe in and out mindfully and remember, the crisis of yesterday is often the joke of tomorrow.*

SITUATION: Raising children of any age is a challenging job, and raising teenagers is about as hard as it gets. You are trying to think of ways to connect and expand your relationship with your teenage daughter without alienating her.

WISDOM: *Occasionally saying out loud the thoughts you are thinking can help make a relationship more intimate. "Being yourself" is rare in today's world, and it's often a little scary, but it can be a valuable way to deepen relationships with your friends and family.*

SITUATION: Your teenage children use chat rooms and social sites on the Internet. You are not very versed in this type of technology and activity, and you do worry about the safety of online chat rooms and social sites. More than once, your child has complained about hateful remarks someone has written anonymously on her personal page on a social site.

WISDOM: *Be conscious and aware that while technology has the power to harness the wisdom of the crowd, unfortunately, it also has the ability to intensify its hatred.*

SITUATION: You are concerned about the amount of nudity your teenagers are exposed to in the media. Between magazines, television, movies, and the Internet, there are many opportunities for them to see naked bodies. You do not consider yourself a prude, but you do wonder about the consequences of all this exposure.

WISDOM: *Enjoy natural sensory desires in mindful ways. Sexuality and sexual intimacy should be a blessing of love and commitment and harm no one. Find ways to express this to your teenagers.*

SITUATION: You usually lose battles with your wife and teenage daughter over what is appropriate clothing to wear out. You are more conservative than them, and you view the clothing your daughter picks out as too sexy for her age. They call you a square and tell you to get with it.

WISDOM: *Don't allow your thoughts to have power over you. Acknowledge that the contents of your thoughts are not facts. You can shape your world through the wisdom of mindful awareness and insight.*

SITUATION: Your teenage daughter is having a difficult time over a breakup with a boyfriend. You have a lot going on in your life between work, your spouse, and other children, yet you want to be there for your daughter in her time of need.

WISDOM: *A great way to demonstrate love to another person is to be completely present for that person.*

SITUATION: Your son wants to negotiate the purchase of his new car by himself. He is so excited about the purchase that he doesn't pay as much attention to the contract as he should. The interest rate he is paying on the car is higher than the going rate, and the extended warranty coverage is too expensive. The dealership has obviously taken advantage of his inexperience at deal making.

WISDOM: *Let the whole world become your teacher. You can learn even from a negative experience. Remain in the present moment with attention and wake up to the sacredness and magic of every second in your life.*

SITUATION: Every time you get the cell phone bill, you just scratch your head at the amount of time your teenage children spend instant messaging. Because of the telephone plan you are on, it's not a money issue, but it makes you wonder if constant connectivity is healthy for them.

WISDOM: *Because speech is so predominant in our lives, and because our words are so consequential, learning the art of skillful communication needs to be a significant aspect of our practice.*

SITUATION: Raising teenage children is hard enough. One of your teens is not fond of school, and she's not doing homework or getting good grades. You are trying to determine the most effective way to punish her.

WISDOM: *Do not think that because you are suffering you can speak harshly, retaliate, or punish others. Breathe in and remember your Buddha nature, your capacity for calm and compassion.*

SITUATION: Anyone who has a teenage child understands how challenging it can be to raise them. The curfew you set for your two teenage children is being ignored, and you are tired of always being the bad guy. So instead of constantly fighting about this issue, you decide to have a family meeting to resolve it.

WISDOM: *Dealing with the unexpected is an opportunity to practice patience and nonaggression.*

SITUATION: You try not to be a snoop, especially when it comes to your teenage children. But the other day, you came across something disturbing. While you were putting some clothes away for your 17-year-old daughter, you noticed a birth control dispenser in her drawer. Once you fathomed what this meant, you weren't sure what to do. So far you have not mentioned it to anyone.

WISDOM: *Take a few deep breaths. Becoming aware of your breath helps you calm the mind because you are reflecting on the present moment.*

SITUATION: One of your children has rejected the religion they were brought up in and has decided to practice another one. You want them to go back to your religion.

WISDOM: *Love means little if your major way of expressing it is to pressure others to conform to your views of how they should be or what they should do. It's more unfortunate if you have no awareness of what you are doing and how it is perceived by others.*

SITUATION: You and your daughter, who is taking Philosophy 101 in college, have one of the most pleasant discussions ever. In her class, they are discussing whether life is real or a dream. You admire the development of her wisdom and knowledge. You see her like a butterfly who has just spread her wings and gained freedom.

WISDOM: *Connection is your true nature; you just have to learn to permit it.*

SITUATION: Your oldest child is going to be graduating from high school this year and will then go off to college. It's going to be a difficult adjustment for you. You don't want his high school years to end.

WISDOM: *Impermanence is a principle of harmony. When you do not struggle against it, you are in harmony with reality. You must use every precious moment. Be aware of impermanence and appreciate the enormous potential of your human existence.*

SITUATION: Your daughter did not get into the college of her choice. It is making you a little depressed. You thought this college would be perfect for her. So much time and energy was spent going through the application and interview process that you feel drained.

WISDOM: *Mindful meditation can help treat depression. Achieve focused awareness of what is happening moment to moment by observing your breathing. Allow stray thoughts or emotions that enter the mind to pass, and return your attention to your breathing.*

SITUATION: Being a fairly good judge of character, you can't help but feel concerned when your son brings his college girlfriend home for a holiday visit. She does not look like any of his previous girlfriends. You are afraid that she will influence your son to do things outside of his character.

WISDOM: *The judging mind has an opinion about everyone and everything. Judging people produces no good consequences and causes pain and suffering. It is merely an old habit filled with old learning, and it is a waste of time. Become aware of when your mind is judging. If you acknowledge it without giving it open, clear attention, the judging mind begins to dissolve itself.*

SITUATION: After years of sacrificing for your children, you are ready to embrace your freedom now that the last one is graduating from college. You decide to start doing some good things for yourself. You enjoyed sacrificing for your children so that they could all go to college debt-free, and you're happy that they all took you up on your offer. But now you want to change your life a little and do some good things just for yourself.

WISDOM: *Do not count on receiving credit for your good deeds. Rejoice in your good deeds and also in whatever life gives you. Do not crave otherwise. Know that whatever you have been given is for your own highest good. See for yourself what brings contentment, clarity, and peace.*

SITUATION: Your child is going through a rough time after graduating from college. It seems like he is stuck in low gear and will not move out of it to begin the next phase of his life. You have talked to him at great length about what his next move will be. You just don't know how to begin teaching him about adult life.

WISDOM: *While the relationship between a student and a teacher is important, it is only one part of the training, awakening, and understanding of the mind. The student needs to do the training that the teacher offers. It cannot be done for him. The student must see and experience for himself.*

SITUATION: You are in high school, and your parents are getting a divorce. The whole process has turned into such a mess that you cannot stand it anymore. You are so angry at your parents for putting you through this. You want to know why they could not suck it up and put off the divorce for a few years until you finish high school.

WISDOM: *When you are angry with someone, you may think you are seeing them clearly, but you are not. Anger paints people with negativity, so you are actually seeing the person or that situation through distorted lenses.*

SITUATION: You find out by accident that you were adopted. As you try to pick yourself off the floor after hearing this news, your head is spinning. You are stunned, shocked, disappointed, frustrated, confused, angry, and a host of other emotions that you did not know you were capable of feeling. It's as if your whole world just fell apart.

WISDOM: *Since your happiness or unhappiness depends on your actions, you should feel empowerment because you are in control of your actions. You are not, however, in charge of what others do or have done. You can choose to be happy in spite of learning this news since you had and have no control over what happened.*

SITUATION: You learn that you were adopted at an early age. You love your adoptive parents more than anything and appreciate the sacrifice they made for you. Recently, you've learned that your birth mother is trying to make contact with you.

WISDOM: *Meditation siphons off the pools of old collected experience, allowing you to act skillfully and compassionately in the present, instead of reacting to the past. Let go, forgive, and accept.*

SITUATION: You are angry with your parents because they are overprotective. You are entering the summer before college, and you expect them to trust you more and give you a little more freedom. In the fall, they will not have much of a say in what you can and cannot do, but you want to feel that they respect you as an adult now.

WISDOM: *Parenting is one of the most difficult jobs in the world. A parent never really knows if they are doing a good job. They can only hope. In most cases, parents try to protect their children because of their love for them. So if you get angry with your parents, do so with a heart of kindness. They are trying.*

SITUATION: Your younger brother, who is not legal drinking age, gets caught drinking with his friends and receives a light punishment from your parents. When you did the same thing last year, you got a severe punishment. You blame your parents for this unfair punishment and feel angry at them and your brother.

WISDOM: *It is always easier to blame someone else for your problems and hurt feelings than to acknowledge that there may be a fundamental wrongness in your own view.*

SITUATION: This is going to be a tight year for holiday presents because of your mother's tenuous job situation. You want to make sure you ask for things that you truly need in order to help out so the holidays are fun and not marred by pressure to fulfill your desires.

WISDOM: *Try creating a 30-day list. Write down what you want. Thirty days later, try to remember what is on that list. Do you still want or need it? When wishes are few, the heart is happy.*

SITUATION: You are so angry with your parents. All your friends are going to a concert festival, but your parents say you cannot go. They give you their reasons, but it still just boils down to the fact that they do not trust you. You feel that you have given them no reason to feel this way.

WISDOM: *Getting angry at someone will never make you feel better in the long term.*

SITUATION: Your dad has a great career opportunity available to him. Unfortunately, it means that you will have to move to a new state. At this stage of high school, you really do not want to move. You are very angry with your parents because they are not including you in the decision-making process.

WISDOM: *If you are angry at a person, that person is not the problem. Your anger is the problem. No matter how much you think the anger is coming from the other person, it is not. You cannot blame the other person for your anger.*

SITUATION: You want to try parachuting, but you need your parents to sign a form because of your age. They will not sign it, saying they are afraid for your safety. You're so upset that you react in an angry way.

WISDOM: *When you are angry or upset about something that someone did to you, if you pause and take a breathing break—three deep, conscious breaths—you will discover many other options available to you and react in a better way, without anger.*

SITUATION: Your parents do not trust one of your friends, who has a tattoo and body piercing and got in a bit of trouble not too long ago. You keep trying to tell your parents that your friend has changed her ways and that the tattoo and body piercing are just ways of expressing herself, but they still do not trust her. You feel you are old enough to choose your own friends. This is creating tension, frustration, and resentment in your relationship with your parents.

WISDOM: *To reduce resentment in your life, practice exhaling your tensions and frustrations like smoke and inhaling clear and blissful light.*

SITUATION: Your parents want you to go to college right after high school. But you want to take a year off and do some traveling before you go to college.

WISDOM: *Paths cannot be taught, they can only be taken.*

SITUATION: Your child thinks you do not understand anything. She says she is in love and feels mature enough for a sexual relationship.

WISDOM: *Parenting is a practice, and even good parents don't understand all the time and make mistakes, too. Parents who consume mindfully, who tread the middle way, and who refrain from unhealthy excess will encourage their children to learn and exercise similar self-control.*

Relatives

SITUATION: Talking about politics with your father is always frustrating and makes you feel angry. No matter what you say, you can never convince him to change his political views.

WISDOM: *These feelings do not mean that you should not talk about social problems or political issues. In such a conversation, just being mindful and speak with a compassionate mind and heart.*

SITUATION: You feel that your brother's girlfriend is taking advantage of him. He asks your advice about possibly asking his girlfriend to marry him.

WISDOM: *When giving advice to others, have compassion and thoughts for their benefit.*

SITUATION: After you informed an aging parent, who still had their wits about them, that they would have to go into a nursing home, the parent passed away. The grief you experience is greater because the parent did not want to leave their house to go into the nursing home.

WISDOM: *Heal your grief and sorrows by being compassionate to yourself. You did the best you could.*

SITUATION: Even though you are grown up, it bothers you when your mother's volatile temper erupts.

WISDOM: *When another person makes you suffer, it is because she suffers deeply within herself and her suffering is spilling over. She doesn't need punishment; she needs help.*

SITUATION: One of your favorite uncles has a drinking problem that is negatively affecting your entire family.

WISDOM: *Ask the uncle to help you understand. If you can help him remove the roots of suffering within him, he will no longer suffer, and he will stop causing you suffering.*

SITUATION: It seems that at this time in your life you are taking care of a lot of people. You're caring for your children. One of your parents needs help with a medical condition and needs to be driven to the doctor every week for treatment. You seem to be the only one with a flexible enough schedule to help out.

WISDOM: *When you engage in fulfilling the needs of others, your own needs are fulfilled as a byproduct.*

SITUATION: Your family and friends were there for you after a messy divorce, but now you are tired of burdening others with your troubles. Hopefully, the ordeal has given you a new source of strength.

WISDOM: *Take time to be alone on a regular basis. Listen to your heart, check your intentions, reevaluate your goals and your activities.*

SITUATION: Almost every time you see your mother-in-law, she says something that makes your skin crawl. Even though you are very angry, you don't say anything to her because you know it will disturb your husband and upset the family balance.

WISDOM: *Repressing anger is not healthy. The best antidote to anger is loving kindness, to yourself and whoever "made" you angry. Loving kindness develops from realizing that only someone who is unhappy will hurt someone else. Therefore, the person who hurt you cannot be happy, and you should try to feel compassion, not anger, toward them.*

SITUATION: A middle-aged family member has just lost a very good job due to layoffs in difficult economic times. With two children in college, the fear she is experiencing is great.

WISDOM: *You can counter fear by seeing it as a projection and as impermanent.*

SITUATION: Your father recently passed away. Once, a long time ago, he told you that you were ornery and should change. When he said it, you were hurt. Now that he is gone, you are beginning to understand that maybe he was right.

WISDOM: *Work continuously on your unfinished business. When you wake each morning, start the day by reaffirming your intention to practice loving kindness and compassion. Remind yourself each day to work at letting go of ego clinging, selfishness, controlling behavior, negative thoughts, possessiveness, aggression, resentment, and confusion. Resolve each day to find one small way that you can change a frozen behavior pattern, and try to do so.*

264

SITUATION: At a recent holiday party, you got into a big debate with your father-in-law about universal health care coverage. You feel that he is close-minded. In defending your position, you became angry.

WISDOM: *Remain open-minded with a sense of humor around closed-minded people; they think they are right.*

SITUATION: You remember your grandmother as a spunky lady who always had time and love for you when you were growing up. Unfortunately, she is all alone in the last phase of her life. You don't have extra money to help her out financially, but you still want to give her something to make her remaining years pleasant.

WISDOM: *Giving attention is one of the purest expressions of love.*

SITUATION: You have been concerned about your father's happiness since your mother passed away. He has recently met a new romantic partner, which gives you hope that he is finding some happiness. But you are beginning to become a little worried about his seemingly foolish behavior whenever you get together.

WISDOM: *There is a foolish corner in the brain of the wisest men, and love can make the wise look foolish.*

SITUATION: After the death of one of your parents, you are experiencing a deep depression that is hard to shake off.

WISDOM: *Death is not depressing. It is simply a fact of life. If we did not have death, we would not appreciate life.*

SITUATION: Caring for an aging parent and living your own life is proving to be a difficult task. You feel sandwiched and guilty. You love your parent and want them to be happy, but between raising children and caring for your parent, you're not sure which job is more difficult.

WISDOM: *See your parent as a small child, fragile and vulnerable, and breathe in. See the parent's suffering. Smile with love to the small child within your parent and breathe out. You are their gift.*

SITUATION: After 15 years of marriage and two children, your brother and sister-in-law are getting divorced. The messy divorce is becoming a family crisis because so many people are feeling hurt.

WISDOM: *In a time of crisis, simply be present with whatever occurs, fully there, without judgment or prejudice. Again and again, use mindfulness to see whatever it is just as it is.*

SITUATION: Hosting family holiday parties is not your strong suit, but it is your turn this year. You have issues with some of your spouse's family members, and the feelings are mutual. Yet, you want the party to be fun and pleasant for everyone's sake.

WISDOM: *Even without speaking, people who feel angry often create an agitated atmosphere in their homes; family members who pick up on their sighs and rough gestures grow tense and fearful so that they wind up walking on eggshells to avoid a conflict. These things eat away at relationships.*

SITUATION: Your parents live in the same town as you. Whenever one of your children—their grandchildren—has a school event, they feel that it is necessary for them to come and watch it.

WISDOM: *Unskillful communication is a leading cause of family tension and problems. When you are with your family, try giving yourself some mini-occasions to breathe mindfully and relax.*

SITUATION: You have found out that your mother was unfaithful to your father during a difficult time in their marriage. You feel as if you got the wind knocked out of you and cannot understand how your father stayed with her.

WISDOM: *Remember the transforming power of forgiveness. Forgiveness is at the heart of all happiness.*

SITUATION: Your little sister lost her job and is flat broke. She has nowhere to go, so you are letting her stay at your house until she gets her feet back on the ground.

WISDOM: *Generosity is the willingness to give, to share, to let go. Love is the inspiration, and in giving, you feel more love.*

SITUATION: Friends and family do not understand the spiritual direction you are taking, which is different from their belief system. You feel that your beliefs are being attacked and not taken seriously.

WISDOM: *Break out of your box! Drop the limiting image of yourself as a separate, fixed entity. Meditation will help you let down the walls and the fear. You will see that there is nothing to defend and that no one can attack you.*

SITUATION: Growing up, your parents were extremely strict—so strict that their discipline became a joke among your few friends. You were a good child growing up and never deserved to be treated that way. It was not until college that you were finally able to spread your wings. The resentment has stayed with you into adulthood and still has a negative impact on your relationship with your parents.

WISDOM: *Weigh the advantages of forgiveness and resentment. Then choose.*

SITUATION: Ever since you can remember, the sibling rivalry in your family has been intense. When you were young, it seemed to be around sports and schoolwork. But now that you all are adults, it has taken a weird turn and often erupts into fights among siblings, who then do not talk to each other for months on end.

WISDOM: *How can you quarrel, knowing that life is as fleeting as a rainbow, a flash of lightning, a star at dawn?*

SITUATION: You get off the phone with your mother after a huge fight. Your face is red, your heart is pounding, and your mind is racing with mean thoughts. Things have been building for a while because she is trying to get too involved with decisions you are making in your life. She said one thing that just set you off, and you lost your cool completely.

WISDOM: *Becoming aware of every body sensation, sound, and mood as it unfolds in the moment helps you control attention and better face troubling thoughts. Endure the anger or sadness and let it pass without ruminating or trying to change the feeling.*

SITUATION: You were a single child who grew up with reserved parents, but married into a large, culturally diverse family. Whenever there is a family function or party involving your spouse's family, you feel like you don't fit into the group.

WISDOM: *Everyone is vulnerable in life. We need each other, and you need to keep your support system in good repair because we are all interconnected to each other. By acknowledging your vulnerability and reliance on other people, you begin to contain and experience your feelings so you can become fully yourself.*

SITUATION: Your parents divorced when you were young, and there was not a whole lot of love in your home life after that. Both of your parents were bitter with each other, and a lot of that bitterness was directed at you. This experience has had a major impact on you in your relationship with yourself and those you love.

WISDOM: *You can search the entire universe for someone more deserving of your love than yourself, and that person will not be found. The person you should want most to love you is yourself. When you generate love for yourself first, there is no obstacle to feeling love for others as well.*

SITUATION: Since retirement, your parents seem to be living a college lifestyle. While you applaud them for staying active, it is a little embarrassing to watch them at parties and family functions. They are wearing clothes and jewelry that people their age should not be wearing, and the stories they're telling are more appropriate for people in their twenties.

WISDOM: *It is hard to let things be. This makes it difficult to control yourself. So you attempt to control those close to you. In reality, you have absolutely no control over the behavior of others; so allow it instead of trying to control it. Sitting teaches you to allow everything to be as it is. Just sit there and allow everything to do its thing. Let it be.*

SITUATION: You love your parents deeply and appreciate all that they have done for you, but sometimes they try to act a little too cool and just look foolish instead.

WISDOM: *It is skillful to focus on and cultivate the positive in life. Do not blot out the negative, but spend more of your time and energy on the positive.*

SITUATION: Your older sister is the perfect daughter. She has excelled in athletics and school and has never gotten in big trouble. You know that your parents love you, but it has always been difficult to live in her shadow. No matter how hard you've tried, you could not reach her level, and it's often seemed that your parents were comparing you negatively to her.

WISDOM: *Every time you can restore even a small amount of peace within yourself, you have a positive effect on your family.*

SITUATION: When you were young and your parents got divorced, you were raised by your mother. Your father began a new life with a new family. At first he tried to stay connected to you, but as time went by, it became harder for him to spend a lot of time with you. Your feeling of abandonment has created hatred and anger toward him.

WISDOM: *Nothing can help or hurt you as much as the thoughts you carry in your head. You can often balance hatred or anger by developing thoughts of compassion and forgiveness.*

SITUATION: Your parents are getting a divorce. While overhearing one of their arguments, you realize they are blaming you for some of their problems.

WISDOM: *Even when your world crumbles, you can use it as an opportunity to awaken. Whether through illness or hardship, sometimes life takes an unpredictable path and causes suffering. Instead of embracing fear, face these circumstances with dignity and grace. You have limited power and control over many aspects of life.*

SITUATION: Your father-in-law sometimes says things that can be construed as anti-Semitic. You get angry at him when you hear him say such things.

WISDOM: *Love is the ultimate way to transform people, even those who are full of hatred. Love is the only answer to hatred. Hatred never ceases by hatred. By love alone it is healed.*

SITUATION: You have made it a habit not to download any files that are sent to you as email attachments. Your computer has been infected by viruses a couple of times, and you are not taking any chances. Family and friends don't understand your logic and get a little upset with you when they send you files to download.

WISDOM: *Whatever you are doing, be observant, careful, and alert. Put the dough in the oven and watch it.*

SITUATION: Your sister is giving you the silent treatment because she is very angry with you over something you did not do to help out one of your parents. You have apologized to her and to your parent, but she is still very angry and will not talk to you.

WISDOM: *Anger distorts the truth by making you believe you are good and the other person is bad. You can't see any good qualities in another person when you're angry with them. This is not a helpful way to look at a conflict.*

SITUATION: Your parents are in a major fight, each upset and angry with the other person. They have not told you what the fight is about, and you realize that it's none of your business. Even though you are an adult now, you are still very concerned about their relationship and want to help.

WISDOM: *When a heart and mind are filled with hate and anger, there is no room left for compassion or loving kindness. The reverse is also true: if a heart and mind are filled with compassion and loving kindness, there is no room for hate or anger.*

SITUATION: The siblings in your family are fighting over the medical care for your father. He has an terminal illness and does not have long to live. You cannot agree about the best way to handle his remaining days. Each person feels he or she is right, and you're all angry at each other, adding more pressure to an already tense situation.

WISDOM: *Anger never has the effect on another person that we want it to. It usually just makes them angry at us in return.*

SITUATION: One of your uncles is angry with his brother, and the two do not speak. Family gatherings are not the same since the two brothers had their fight. Everyone in the family is suffering because of this feud. You especially feel sorry for your grandparents, who are older and appear to be hurt the most.

WISDOM: *Anger damages you, not the other person. It's you who are red in the face, you who are shouting and making a scene, you who look ridiculous and feel miserable. When you let go of anger, love arises.*

SITUATION: You recently found out that your great-grandfather did some very bad things to people during a war. Even though you were not alive yet during his lifetime and never met the man, you feel hurt and ashamed by his actions.

WISDOM: *When you see things as they are, that is freedom. See the impermanence of life. See the constant flow of pleasant and painful events that are beyond your control. See it all as it is.*

SITUATION: After telling your mother you are planning to make your marriage announcement, she says you are too young to marry and should enjoy your life before you settle down. You are hurt by her words because you know she married young and her marriage seemed to work. You are in love and ready for the next step.

WISDOM: *If you keep compassion alive in you while listening, anger and irritation cannot arise. Learn to listen with only one purpose: to allow the other person to express herself and find relief from her suffering.*

SITUATION: After coming home from college for the summer, you notice that your younger sister is borrowing your clothes without asking. You have gained independence at school, and you really don't want someone wearing your clothes without permission. You try telling her nicely, but she still borrows your clothes. You lock your clothes in a trunk so she cannot get to them.

WISDOM: *All actions have consequences. When someone's actions are thoughtless, you may react in a mean way. When you are mean-spirited or harmful, you experience guilt, confusion, and regret.*

SITUATION: You love your parents deeply and appreciate how much they have done for you, but you are tired of hand-me-down clothes from your older sisters. You want new clothes that you pick out yourself.

WISDOM: *The deepest happiness occurs when you let go of what is unnecessary, like accumulating material possessions and new experiences.*

SITUATION: You love your brother, but you feel jealous of him, too. It seems like everything comes easier to him than you. While you struggle with life, he seems to flow through it easily and as happy as a clam.

WISDOM: *Treating someone with loving kindness is the all-purpose antidote to dealing with your own jealousy. Refrain from watering the seed of jealousy. Happiness is not possible unless you are free from jealousy.*

SITUATION: It was always a family joke that you were the best mistake your parents ever made. Your siblings are 18 and 20 years older than you are. Because of the age difference, you were never really close to them. They were busy with their own families when you were still very young. Recently, though, both your parents passed away, and you want to forge a better relationship with your siblings.

WISDOM: *Spend today bringing happiness to yourself and your family.*

SITUATION: Your grandmother is all alone since her husband died. You have seen a steady decline in her mental state since your grandfather's death. Although you are busy with your own life, you want to help out in some way.

WISDOM: *Small, simple actions can have big impacts. Even the mere act of being present for someone who is suffering can have a big impact and make a difference in your life and theirs.*

SITUATION: Your grandmother is nearing the end of her life. Unfortunately, the last part of her life has been filled with unbearable physical pain, and she has become so needy that it is putting a strain on everyone in your family.

WISDOM: *Life is so hard, how can we be anything but kind? The practices of mindfulness and loving kindness help us to understand that all things deserve care—that when we relate to all things with kindness, we are relating to ourselves with kindness.*

SITUATION: Your mother had some psychological issues that she was not able to deal with effectively when you were growing up. Now, as you look back at your childhood, you do not have many fond memories of it. You love your mother, but you vow not to do to your children what she did to you. When you think about it, you realize she taught you how not to be and act.

WISDOM: *There are so many teachers in this world because we are all so different and learn in so many different ways. Let everyone and every situation be a teacher for you. An enemy and bad situation can be just as effective at teaching you as a friend and a good situation.*

SITUATION: Your relationship with your mother-in-law is the classic one that comedians joke about, but to you it is no laughing matter. You don't feel that she has the right to intrude on your family's life the way she does. Whenever you question what your mother-in-law is doing in relation to your husband, he gets angry with you. In frustration, he tells you that she is his mother and asks, "What do you expect me to do?" You wish that both your mother-in-law and your husband would be a bit more reasonable.

WISDOM: *You achieve balance and freedom when you learn how to be with your life as it is, not as you would like it to be.*

SITUATION: While you are out with your daughter and grandchild, your daughter punishes her child in what you think is an inappropriate way. You want to say something, but you know it will cause trouble between you and your daughter. So you think it best just to keep your mouth shut.

WISDOM: *Be quiet and let your actions speak for you.*

SITUATION: When your mother got sick and needed a lot of care, your family and some close friends helped you out tremendously. Your husband pitched in at home like never before. The kids helped out with school lunches and other meals, allowing you to spend time with your mother when she needed you. Close friends took over some carpools and errands. You will always appreciate what they did for you. It was truly a gift.

WISDOM: *Even the smallest action done with loving appreciation of life can touch other human beings in a profound way. Appreciating one's life generates a courageous heart and mind.*

SITUATION: Being in the "sandwich generation" brings its own set of issues. Keeping track of both your children and your parents is an exhausting job. But through experience, you realize that you need to talk about issues before they happen so everyone will be comfortable with decisions that must be made. You are trying to talk to your parents and in-laws about setting up living wills—never an easy or comfortable task, but a necessary one.

WISDOM: *When it is difficult to make a decision, pause before acting. Ask yourself, "Is this action skillful and wholesome?" If the action will cause harm to yourself or someone else, do not do it. If the action will cause no harm to yourself or anyone else, then do it and enjoy it.*

SITUATION: You would have to say that your aunt and uncle are about the nicest people you have ever met—and not just because they are related to you. They both go to church on a regular basis, they volunteer their time for local charities, they even take in foster children to give them a new beginning. Unfortunately, one of their own children, your cousin, died in a terrible car accident. They are devastated by the event.

WISDOM: *No one in life leaves without having suffered.*

SITUATION: You witness your granddaughter throwing a tantrum in public. In your opinion, her mother—your daughter-in-law—handles the situation poorly.

WISDOM: *Acknowledge your feelings so they can pass. Every little thing is not your problem.*

SITUATION: Your spouse has confided in you that she had an unhappy childhood because her older brother died in a car accident and her parents never overcame the pain from his death. Life in the house was filled with suffering after her brother died, and your wife does not have too many fond memories from then on.

WISDOM: *A person who lives happily in the present moment is not imprisoned by the past or sucked up by the future. Living in the present moment will provide nourishment to help heal, as well as strength and wisdom to help deal with problems.*

SITUATION: After burying one of your parents last month, you are putting the final touches on your daughter's wedding. You were so looking forward to this wedding because your daughter happily included you in the planning of the event, creating an opportunity for the two of you to bond more deeply. But since your parent passed away, much of the fun of the wedding has vanished for you. You are trying to hold it together for your daughter's sake, but it is hard because you feel so down.

WISDOM: *When you realize the rare and precious opportunity of life, you become a better human being—calmer, gentler, wiser, more motivated, more compassionate, and more balanced.*

SITUATION: Your father is like a friend to you. Even if he were not your father, you suspect that the two of you would be friends. Talking has always been easy for you and him. As he ages, you notice a theme developing in his conversations with you. There seems to be a little regret about things he wishes he had done. It opens your eyes a little about how you want to lead the rest of your life. You don't want to experience these same regrets.

WISDOM: *Everyone alive is eventually going to die. Everyone has a limited time here. The motivation in life should be to figure out the best way to live while you are alive. The best antidote to death is life.*

SITUATION: You have always thought it would be cool to discover an old book written by a family member explaining the family history through their eyes. You never find one, so you decide to create your own for your future generations to find. You enjoy every minute of writing this book. After completing it, you plan to place it in your safe deposit box for your grandchildren.

WISDOM: *Like all humans, you have unlimited capacity to do anything you want when you put your mind to it. If you do not utilize this capacity, it is a lost opportunity for you and the world.*

SITUATION: When your grandfather is dying in the hospital, you visit him to say goodbye. You've always thought of him as your wisest relative. When you walk into the room, his eyes are shut and he is moving his lips making words, but you cannot hear what he is saying. Then he opens his eyes to greet you. You ask what he is saying, and he tells you that every day he reminds himself how special and magical life is. Later, you try to find words to remind yourself of the same sentiment.

WISDOM: *Health is the greatest gift, contentment the greatest wealth, faithfulness the best relationship.*

SITUATION: When your grandmother passed away, she left you a piece of heirloom jewelry in her will. You have kept it, but you never wear it because it's not your style of jewelry. When you showed it to a friend, she asked its value, so you started wondering and brought it to a jewelry store to get it appraised. The jeweler appraised it at an incredibly high value and offered to purchase it. That one piece of jewelry would cover the cost of the new kitchen that you have been saving for.

WISDOM: *Acknowledging that you and everyone you love will die, cherish the blessings that appear in your life and those with whom you share them.*

SITUATION: Your granddaughter is coming down to Florida to visit you with her boyfriend. Your daughter has informed you that the granddaughter is living with the boyfriend now and wants to sleep in the same bed during their visit. You do not feel comfortable with this type of arrangement.

WISDOM: *Mindfully open your heart in loving acceptance of those you cherish. Give them the gift of attentive presence and strengthen your connectedness.*

SITUATION: It is a difficult conversation you plan to have with your parents. They are getting up in years, and as far as you know, they do not have living wills. You don't want to hurt their feelings by bringing up this topic, but you also know that you are the one who will be in charge if something happens to them, and you want to make sure you carry out their wishes.

WISDOM: *Avoid attachment in emotion and you avoid sadness and fear. Remember that even a happy life cannot be without a measure of darkness, and the word "happiness" would lose its meaning if it were not balanced by sadness.*

SITUATION: Your parents still live in the house where you grew up. Back then, the town was considered a nice place to live and raise a family. You have fond memories of your childhood town. Recently, though, you have read reports about a dramatic increase in crime there. You are concerned about your parents' safety. You would like to see them move to a safer area, but it looks like they have no intention of doing that.

WISDOM: *There is pain that is inevitable for all, but much other suffering is optional. Your parents may be wiser than you in taking precautions but not worrying unnecessarily. Painful experiences are inevitably part of life. Use mindfulness and do not embellish the news stories to increase your suffering or cause suffering for your loved ones.*

SITUATION: Your cousin has bipolar disorder. You do not feel comfortable inviting him to family functions because of his unpredictable behavior. You feel bad about it, but you also want to protect your family.

WISDOM: *Make kindness your religion, and it will spread to others. Kindness breeds kindness. First, be compassionate with yourself for feeling this way. When you are experiencing difficult emotions, hold them gently. Then you are likely to do acts of kindness toward others. Mindfully cultivate compassion and understanding for yourself so that through kindness you can add happiness, not pain, to the lives of others.*

SITUATION: As your mother ages, her arthritis seems to be worsening. She is doing no physical exercise to help her condition. It is almost like she has given up. Most days she just lays in bed or on the couch watching television. It is even difficult to get her to come to family functions. You know that if she exercised and tried harder, her life would improve even though she has a physical disorder.

WISDOM: *Try not to focus on the external indicators of aging. You will overlook the internal treasures accumulated with the experiences of a lifetime. Greet the changing seasons of life with joy and faith, aware that all is just as it should be.*

SITUATION: You were surprised to be in your aunt's will. While you were somewhat close to her, you did not think you were any closer than her other nieces and nephews. You are the only one to inherit money. You feel strange about this and your cousins are jealous.

WISDOM: *When envy or jealousy arises, mindfully cut through the storytelling, whether it is yours or others'. Letting go of the suffering that these stories generate, you will see things as they are. Jealousy and envy make people miserable and do not change situations. You can release your feelings of entitlement and by doing that, show others the way.*

Self

SITUATION: You get up in the morning and raise the blinds or open the curtains, somewhat in a fog.

WISDOM: *Before you get up, take some time to reflect on what it means to wake up and meet the day.*

SITUATION: It has been a weekend of playing house catch-up. Much needed outside work was accomplished, but there was a price to pay. Your body is a little sore on Monday morning.

WISDOM: *As you prepare to start your day, envision a large, happy lion stretching and roaring. Raise your arms and spread them wide, palms forward. Stretch. Breathe. Like the lion, leap forward into your day.*

SITUATION: After giving birth to your children, you gained weight. You used the excuse of stress for not changing your eating habits. Your children are getting older and becoming less dependent on you, yet you still can't seem to lose the weight that you gained.

WISDOM: *You need repeated discipline and training to let go of old habits of mind and find new ways of seeing and living.*

SITUATION: You don't like the way you look. After three children, it is very difficult for you to lose the weight that you gained during pregnancy. Whenever the family is together for holidays or special occasions, you shy away from the camera because you do not want to be reminded what you look like in photographs.

WISDOM: *Be happy with the way you look. Preoccupation with your body's appearance or wishing to be thinner does not help you heal. These internal struggles and your idea of perfection just lead to suffering. It is what is inside of you that really counts.*

SITUATION: You recently gave birth. While your health and that of the baby are fine, you are having difficulty losing the weight that you put on during the pregnancy. Other people you know who have had babies lost the weight they had gained by this time. You are beginning to feel pressure from yourself and others.

WISDOM: *Practice letting go of complaints about your body. You have to accept yourself as you are before you can really change. By intentionally cultivating acceptance, you create preconditions for healing. You are much more likely to know what to do and have the inner conviction to act when you have a clear picture of what is actually happening instead of when your vision is clouded by judgments, desires, fears, and prejudices.*

SITUATION: Waking up in the morning, you already feel tired. Your mood is down as you begin thinking about all the things you have to do and all the problems you have to deal with.

WISDOM: *When you awake in the morning, stretch your arms to the sky and breathe deeply. Fill your insides with the emptiness around you.*

SITUATION: Life's pressures have been getting to you lately. You want to begin today the best way possible.

WISDOM: *Make it a point to be happy, to be here and now. The first thought of the day should be positive and special.*

SITUATION: Although you have so many clothes, you can't seem to find anything to wear today.

WISDOM: *Buy less clothing. Buy looser, freer clothing. Give away some of the clothing you do not wear.*

SITUATION: It seems like you are on a hamster wheel every day, and you take life for granted. You want to change this and get your daily priorities straight.

WISDOM: *Start rearranging priorities instead of taking life for granted. Learn to find joy in everything you do and in every interpersonal contact.*

SITUATION: You moved to a new town because of a new job. It feels like a new beginning. You have the perfect opportunity to set new priorities for your life.

WISDOM: *Reflect on what is truly of value, what gives meaning to life. Set your priorities based on that.*

SITUATION: The holidays are fast approaching, and you have not begun to do all that needs to be done. Nervousness and pressure are beginning to set in.

WISDOM: *Before you go to bed, start a list of things you have been putting off.*

SITUATION: Today, you are healthy and happy. It feels so good you want to share it with others.

WISDOM: *Loving thoughts and actions are clearly beneficial for your physical and mental health. They express your true nature.*

SITUATION: Lately, it is hard to get out of bed and do anything. Everything seems to require so much effort that it is becoming difficult to maintain a job and friends. This is more than just the blues; it may be full-fledged depression.

WISDOM: *When you are caught in a powerful depression, or when you are feeling as though there is not much point to anything, it is the time to make the effort required to work with very difficult mind states.*

SITUATION: The number and frequency of worldwide natural disasters is having a paralyzing effect on you. Your sense of powerlessness is overwhelming.

WISDOM: *The emotional patterns in which you feel the most stuck and powerless are the places that invite the greatest patience, compassion, and transformation.*

SITUATION: After a pleasant conversation with a close friend who is going through some major challenges in her life, you begin to pay more attention to your lifestyle and habits. You begin to question the things—TV, Internet, shopping, talking, alcohol—you use to escape the reality of life.

WISDOM: *Pay close attention to your motivations and intentions, asking yourself "why?" before you watch TV, drink alcohol, or indulge in other forms of escapism.*

SITUATION: Noise and activity surround you. With so many distractions, no wonder it is almost impossible to concentrate on work and family.

WISDOM: *You can learn to control your mind so that it is calm and constant. Your mind will be quiet and stable even though you are in the midst of a noisy world.*

SITUATION: You just moved into a new town because of a job transfer. You have not developed any friendships yet, and you're feeling a little overwhelmed and lonely for want of a support system.

WISDOM: *No one can help you as much as your own compassionate thoughts.*

SITUATION: The last time you looked in the mirror, it was very upsetting to see that you were losing your hair quickly.

WISDOM: *Consider the problem within a larger context. Imagine you are in outer space, seeing the problem from there. Or imagine yourself as a bird soaring, looking down at the problem far below. It will likely seem insignificant on this scale, and your anxiety about it should diminish. Return to earth ready to face the problem.*

SITUATION: Tough night last night. The baby kept you awake most of the night crying. You have an important work meeting today, and you feel exhausted as you get out of bed.

WISDOM: *In the shower, rid yourself of impurities and feel the energy of the water. Let the water take you back to the moment of your birth and feel a deep-seated sense of renewal. As the water cascades down your body, let it carry away discomfort and distress, leaving you refreshed and invigorated.*

SITUATION: You have your routine down pretty well. You go to work, eat lunch, come home from work, fix dinner, watch television, get ready for bed. It is a pretty comfortable life.

WISDOM: *Too much comfort weakens the mind and body. Evolve beyond the "little you" who continually seeks zones of comfort.*

SITUATION: After a busy day, nothing feels better than to climb into bed and read a good book. Unfortunately, you keep falling asleep as you read because you are so tired.

WISDOM: *When reading, try stopping every half hour. Close your eyes for a minute or so and bring your attention back to your breath. Feel your mind and body recharge.*

SITUATION: Time is going by so quickly that it is a little frightening. The kids are getting older, your parents are getting older, and you are getting older. It feels as if life is passing you by.

WISDOM: *It is better to embrace a moment than it is to fear the moment passing by. Grab happiness in the passing moments of life.*

SITUATION: Life is going great. This frightens you a little because you are waiting for it to change, for something to go wrong.

WISDOM: *Suffering is actually essential to happiness. You have to know being too cold to appreciate being warm.*

SITUATION: There is a lot of talk these days about new ways to discover happiness that are simple and easy. You are a little suspicious because most of these new methods involve charging you money.

WISDOM: *Get rid of the false, and you will automatically realize the true.*

SITUATION: As you gain more wisdom and increase your happiness by taking steps to simplify your life, you feel you want to go even further and develop a vision and mission for yourself.

WISDOM: *A mission and personal vision are necessary. Write down what is most important to you, what you believe is most fundamental to being your best self and finding peace with yourself.*

SITUATION: Life is going pretty well for you. You have a healthy family, a good job, a nice house. But you just don't feel happy. You really want to change that and feel more happiness.

WISDOM: *Ask yourself: "What am I waiting for to make me happy? Why am I not happy right now?" Every moment is an opportunity to water the seeds of happiness in yourself. If you develop the capacity to be happy in any surroundings, you will be able to share your happiness with others.*

SITUATION: Taking the next step to personal growth is always fun and exciting. You are at a point in your life where you want to try to figure out what is important. You want to try to figure out the answers to the big questions of life.

WISDOM: *In trying to figure out what is important in life, a good first step is to figure out what is not important in life. This puts the big picture of life in a better perspective.*

SITUATION: Every time you look in the mirror, the first thing you notice is your imperfect nose. If only you could get that little bump fixed, you think, your life would be so much better.

WISDOM: *There is no such thing as perfection in the human body. Imperfections have a beauty of their own.*

SITUATION: When you read a book, your mind seems to wander all over the place. You find that you have to read the same paragraph two or sometimes three times before you get the meaning of it.

WISDOM: *Being grounded means having your attention completely inside your body no matter what you are doing. When you are completely attentive, you are grounded.*

SITUATION: You are having trouble falling asleep and sleeping well throughout the night because you cannot stop thinking about all the things on your mind. Between work, the economy, and family responsibilities, it is a stressful time in your life, and the lack of sleep is making things worse.

WISDOM: *If you make a commitment to be fully awake when you are awake, your view of not being able to sleep at certain times will change with your view of everything else.*

SITUATION: After your mother passes away, it seems like you cannot stop thinking about death. Whenever you find yourself alone, you become frightened by your thoughts of death. What happens when you die? What would happen to your children if you died? What if another important person in your life died now?

WISDOM: *Death is always here. It exists. Try not to forget this. When you keep death at your fingertips, you become less involved, less compulsive about the satisfaction or gratification of various desires in the moment. When you are not so clouded by desires and fantasies, you're less inclined to hold onto things and more open to love and generosity.*

SITUATION: You have not felt like yourself lately. You can't quite pin it down, but this melancholy feeling is having an effect on your normal activities. You don't feel like going out and socializing with co-workers or friends. You just want to do what you have to do to get by and then stay home alone.

WISDOM: *Your mental health is not defined by the content of your thoughts, but rather by your relationship to the content of your thoughts. You can become disentangled with the definition of yourself. Stop and observe your feelings and thoughts and have compassion for yourself.*

SITUATION: You have gotten over the initial shock of your divorce. Now you want to treat yourself well after the breakup.

WISDOM: *You do not have to look outside yourself to find great happiness. You can find it inside. Your treasure house is in yourself. It contains all you will ever need.*

SITUATION: Your habit of dwelling on things began when you were young. In school, it was upcoming tests and papers. Then as you got older, it was relationships, then jobs and family. Whenever something out of the ordinary comes up, you automatically begin to fixate on it.

WISDOM: *Habitual patterns get stronger when you are on automatic pilot. When you pause and take some deep, conscious breaths, you can break that pattern and allow space into your state of mind.*

SITUATION: You are a sucker for infomercials for exercise equipment. The results they show on television are inspiring, but it seems that after you purchase a piece of exercise equipment, you lose interest in it quickly. You do not get the results that they show on television.

WISDOM: *We get so many things, and after we get them we lose interest in them. It's disconcerting. When you try to satisfy your desires, you increase your wanting. It becomes a vicious circle. Being satisfied with what you already have is a magical golden key to being alive in an inspired way.*

SITUATION: You can spend hours on the Internet and not even realize it. It doesn't matter where you are, because you have at least three devices from which you can access the Internet. You use it for both work and entertainment. It is truly amazing what the Internet can do.

WISDOM: *When the mind is continuously looking for something to entertain it, an unhealthy mental environment is created. This obstacle can distract you from your development and impede your progress. Becoming mindful of the power the Internet can have over you helps you overcome this obstacle and become more appreciative and observant of your life. Remember, everything in moderation.*

SITUATION: Every morning when you wake up, you turn on the television so you can watch the news for 15 minutes before you get out of bed and get ready for work.

WISDOM: *Television news is not for the faint at heart. If you listen to the news, it may seem as if the world is spinning out of control. Combat this feeling by not taking too much in life for granted. Everything you have is a gift.*

SITUATION: Over the past few years, you have let yourself go both physically and mentally. After reaching the bottom, you are trying to pick yourself up by making a list that prioritizes what you want to accomplish both physically and mentally.

WISDOM: *A person cannot live life without having problems. A person cannot successfully run away from problems. But a person can lead a happy life and learn how to live with problems and deal with them.*

SITUATION: Never being one to take risks, you are realizing that life is quickly passing you by.

WISDOM: *Every second turns into a minute. Every minute into an hour. Every hour into a day. Every day into a week. Every week into a month. Every month into a year. Every year into a lifetime. How you spend every second is vitally important. Try not to waste too many opportunities.*

SITUATION: You want to adopt a mantra or personal philosophy that you can repeat to yourself to stay balanced and mindful.

WISDOM: *Repeat to yourself what you know of the teachings of the Buddha or your understanding of what brings about your happiness. Choose something like "May I be happy just as I am," or "May I be peaceful with whatever is happening."*

SITUATION: Your Facebook page has taken over your life. It is the only thing you can think of and talk about. You get so excited every time you make a change to it that you have to tell all your friends about it. If no friends are around, you start talking about it with your sister. You can find something to say about your page in every conversation you have.

WISDOM: *Give ego a hard time. Instead of listening to the radio or singing in the car or shower, talk to your ego. "Okay, ego, you've been giving me problems my entire life, and now I'm getting smarter. I am not going to be under your sway one more day." Surrender the ego so you can feel your connection to the universe.*

SITUATION: After raising your children and seeing them off to college, you feel brain-dead. The lively battles that went on and kept your brain active no longer happen since the kids have left home. You also find that you have extra time on your hands. You decide to take philosophy classes at an online university.

WISDOM: *Spring-clean your brain, get to know yourself again, and learn how to pay attention.*

SITUATION: Sitting on the couch and flipping through the channels trying to find something on TV is just not doing anything for you. After watching an infomercial for a cardiovascular machine for 15 minutes, you decide that you have had enough. You put the bag of chips away, turn off the TV, put on the walking shoes and head outside for a walk.

WISDOM: *Once you get into the habit of daily exercise of the mind and body, you are bound to think, "How can I not do this every day?"*

SITUATION: You've just realized that you have been thinking about yourself way too much. It seems to be all about you! You think constantly about your troubles, problems, pains, relationships.

WISDOM: *Develop the important skill of thinking about others. When you put others at the center of your life, it releases your natural desire for happiness and liberates you from your self-centeredness while helping you to enlighten your heart.*

SITUATION: You are becoming interested in the teachings of Buddha. Many things within the philosophy of Buddhism make sense to you. You wonder if you have what it takes to develop a Buddhist mind.

WISDOM: *Demonstrate your Buddha nature through compassion and responsiveness, making a commitment to lessen the suffering in the world in any way you can.*

SITUATION: It seems like you have so many desires that all your energy is being zapped by just thinking about them. You want to get married, buy a house, have children, find a better job, get a new car. You just can't stop craving for things in your life to be different and better.

WISDOM: *Putting down the burden of craving will improve your happiness. Freeing yourself from your unquenchable thirst for things and pleasures will give you more energy, creating a refreshing calm in you. Most of the time this is all you have to do to feel better and live a happier life.*

SITUATION: It seems like nothing is going your way. Your life and career are not going according to your plan. You wanted to be married at this point in your life, and you wanted to hold a certain position at work. Neither has come true, and you are beginning to worry, feel sorry for yourself, even panic about it.

WISDOM: *Feeling sorry for yourself or wishing things were different in your life only increases the amount of suffering you experience. Stop wanting things to be different than they are. Try not to struggle or fight with life.*

SITUATION: You seem to have hit a wall in your spiritual progress. You don't know whether your practice is good or bad for you anymore. You want it to have a bigger impact on you than it is having. But you just can't seem to make it to the next level.

WISDOM: *Even in confusing or trying times, it is important to do whatever you can to try to make yourself a better person.*

SITUATION: This year you want your New Year's resolution to mean something. You want your life to improve. You don't just want to resolve to lose weight or get a better job. You want your resolution to be deeper.

WISDOM: *Resolve to achieve freedom, joy, and happiness in life; learn from your mistakes; take responsibility for your actions; and cultivate compassion.*

SITUATION: You have not been getting enough sleep lately because your baby is keeping you awake at night crying. In a meeting at work, you are doing everything you can to stay awake.

WISDOM: *Clarify how you feel with respect to the body, being aware of postures, breath, and the interplay of the physical elements. Become sensitive to just how much food and sleep you actually need.*

SITUATION: Sometimes it feels as if you have no freedom at all. Between children, family, and work, there is never any time left for you. You don't need a lot, but every once in a while you need to feel a little freedom from all your responsibilities.

WISDOM: *To feel contentment in your own life and have respect for others, you must feel humility for yourself.*

SITUATION: You have been hit with writer's block while trying to keep your blog updated. You can't seem to find anything to write about, let alone anything interesting to write about. Writing your blog has always been easy and fun in the past, but now it is a big chore and not much fun.

WISDOM: *Writer's block is just interference. Use the interference to create the words and let them flow and be delivered to the page. Just go from one word to the next.*

SITUATION: You cannot believe it, but you changed the color of your hair from brown to blond, and people are actually looking at you differently and treating you differently. You are still the same person; only your hair has changed.

WISDOM: *Be courageous—not locked into preconceptions of how things are, but courageous enough to be open and receptive to different possibilities.*

SITUATION: Looking at your grades in school and breezing through homework, you know that you are smart. But after seeing your IQ score, you realize how much smarter you are than most people. It feels good to know that you are a genius.

WISDOM: *To become fully awake, one most overcome conceit. When you explore the feelings of superiority in your life and find a way to end them, you allow empathy, loving kindness, wisdom, generosity, compassion, and awakening to enter into your mind and heart.*

SITUATION: When you were maturing, your body developed nicely—except for your breasts. As a teenager, you never wanted to be seen in a swimsuit because your chest was so small. You always felt that your life would be better if your breasts were bigger. You wanted to get surgery to increase their size, but your parents would not allow it. Now that you are an adult, you are thinking about getting breast augmentation surgery.

WISDOM: *As enlightenment grows in you, confusion and ignorance will have to withdraw. It will not only influence your thinking but also your body and your way of living.*

SITUATION: Since your spouse passed away, you have not gone out to dinner or on vacation because you are embarrassed to eat or travel alone. You don't want people to stare at you or feel sorry for you.

WISDOM: *By focusing and living in the present moment, you can change loneliness and discomfort into joy. Treasure life.*

SITUATION: Call it a midlife crisis or disillusionment or any of a number of things, but you feel like you are at a crossroads. Your business career has been rewarding, yet now you want to change careers and move into a field that can help people, like counseling or teaching. You want to give something back to society. Your spouse gives you the okay to make whatever decision will bring you the most happiness.

WISDOM: *You think that if you give up the illusion of control, you'll miss out, lose, fall behind. But giving up something you never had can only clarify your life.*

SITUATION: You were born a worrier. It is in your genes. Your mother is a worrier, and her mother was a worrier. You cannot seem to break this habit, and it annoys you. Sometimes an entire day can be wasted worrying about a silly problem.

WISDOM: *Wasting a whole day caught up in habitual patterns of worry, fear, greed, or jealousy is easy. Instead, look at every day as an opportunity to break these habits and become free. One way to wake up and change habitual patterns is to ask yourself every morning: "What is the most important thing today?"*

SITUATION: In childhood, you had a weight problem. You endured a lot of teasing. Then in college you got the strength to lose your unwanted weight. You have kept the weight off as an adult. Whenever you see a picture of yourself from the past, you wish you could just forget you used to look that way.

WISDOM: *We tend to perceive what we have learned to see. It is based on conditioning and memory. Unless you make a deliberate and conscious effort to see things as they are, you miss many beautiful objects and scenes in life.*

SITUATION: Every morning, the first thing you do when you wake up is to think about all the things you have to do today. It gets your heart racing, and you rush out of bed to begin your busy day. Sometimes, though, you feel so overwhelmed by the number of things you have to do that you just want to hide under the covers.

WISDOM: *Look upon each morning as a rebirth and understand that only this one day exists. Today is your entire life. But that does not mean rushing or doing as many things as you can.*

SITUATION: You are short. The teasing began when you were young and continues to this day. You did not choose this body and can do nothing about it. You know that you have not made teams in school because of your height, and you know that in the business world you have been passed over for promotions because of it. It still upsets you when you are not treated as an equal because of your height.

WISDOM: *In life, there will always be obstacles to overcome, both big and small. Obstacles are part of your spiritual path and offer learning experiences. An obstacle can be a path in and of itself. It can be a message or signal for you to wake up and become aware of what is really going on.*

SITUATION: The hardest thing in the world for you to do is to sit still in silence. Your mind and mouth race at the same speed: fast. While it may be exhausting, it is the way you are built.

WISDOM: *Sometimes the best way to feel your feelings or think your thoughts is to sit in silence. When you do, you are less distracted and can be more fully aware of the essence of your feelings and thoughts. As you look at them more deeply, you give them space to live for a while. Sitting in silence is full of potential wisdom. Feeling uncomfortable or threatened by silence is no excuse for filling all your time with thoughts and words.*

SITUATION: In school, you perfected the art of daydreaming. No matter the subject or time of day, you could switch on a daydream whenever you wanted to. The ability to get lost in fantasy has not left you as you've gotten older. In a meeting at work or doing something with the family, you can still turn on that daydreaming switch.

WISDOM: *Fantasizing or daydreaming in moderation is fine. But don't spend too much time lost in fantasy, oblivious to direct experiences of sight and sound, smell and taste, bodily sensations. Get in touch with these experiences. They are what living is all about.*

SITUATION: Your wedding is only a few weeks away. It is crunch time both emotionally and in terms of the work you have left to do for the wedding. Lack of sleep and high stress are taking their toll on how you are treating other people. Either you are mad at them or they are mad at you.

WISDOM: *When you are always running, it becomes a habit. You struggle all the time, even during your sleep. You are at war within yourself, and you can easily start a war with others.*

SITUATION: You have this great idea for a website. You have been going over it in your head for a long time. You have written information down and talked to people about it. This idea is totally consuming your life. Your spouse will not discuss the idea with you anymore because it is the only thing you talk about. It has become a part of you.

WISDOM: *Attachment to ideas can be a barrier to opening. Ideas are fine; it is the attachment to them or the excessive reliance on them that causes the trouble. Live in a state of constant amazement.*

SITUATION: Only three more years until retirement, and, boy, you cannot wait. The next three years cannot go by quick enough for you. You have prepared yourself both emotionally and financially for retirement and have it all planned out. No more boring meetings or commuting in traffic or incompetent bosses. Your life will be yours again.

WISDOM: *There are pleasures to be had throughout the journey, not just at the end. Find the joy in your life on your journey to retirement. Don't wait.*

SITUATION: "Why am I here?" "Why am I in this body?" "Why am I on this planet?" "Why am I alive at this particular time?" You enjoy thinking about questions like these. Not only do you like to talk about such topics with friends and loved ones, but you also feel it gives your life meaning and importance. You find it challenging and fun to contemplate life like this.

WISDOM: *The only way to truly see the unique richness and magic in life is to understand and believe each moment is important and precious. Life can be lost so easily that we cannot take it for granted.*

SITUATION: The first thing you do when you get home from work is to turn on your computer and check for work emails.

WISDOM: *Everyday activities can be done on autopilot. Instead, choose to attend to them in a different way. Make them into "mindfulness bells" and use them to be fully aware and awake, completely present for the blessings that surround you. The sound of turning the computer on can be a mindfulness bell, and so can the "You've got mail" sound.*

SITUATION: For as long as you can remember, you have wanted to write the "Great American Novel." Every time you've started to write it, though, you've quickly ceased because it was never good enough. This time you are looking at it from a different angle—as a challenge. You vow to write every day for one year and see what comes out. No quitting for 365 days.

WISDOM: *Welcome obstacles, for they are your challenges. Come up against big challenges—and learn how to soften and open. One of the greatest challenges you will face is resisting thoughts that are self-judgmental or tainted with negativity. Instead, open to your capacity to offer loving kindness to yourself during this process.*

SITUATION: Growing up, you kept a diary. Writing about what was happening in your life always helped you to remain balanced, especially during your teen years. In college you stopped keeping your journal for many reasons, and, upon graduating from college and moving, you got rid of your old diaries. Now, with teenage children of your own, you wish you had your diaries back.

WISDOM: *Do not regret the past. Instead of being carried away by your thinking, worries, or anxieties about the future or regrets about the past, dwell fully in the present moment, fully aware of each step you take.*

SITUATION: Two or three times a year, you feel nostalgic about your youth and take out your photographs. It gives you great pleasure to remember all the good times you had. Looking at the old pictures brings you back to a time when life seemed simpler and less confusing and stressful. Seeing the smiling faces of relatives and friends is always a mood booster for you.

WISDOM: *Do not wish to be anything but what you are, where you are, right now. Learn to wish that everything should come to pass exactly as it does.*

SITUATION: You're not an artist, but you recently went to an art museum and looked at a painting that had a tremendous impact on you. You don't quite understand why.

WISDOM: *A writer or artist has an effect on the collective consciousness.*

SITUATION: You are busy getting ready for work when your child enthusiastically comes into the room and wants you to look at the pretty sky out the window.

WISDOM: *Experience all things with the enthusiasm of a child, as if you were seeing them for the first time.*

SITUATION: Maybe this is your midlife crisis. Lately it seems you are looking at your life differently. Things that once were important, like career and money, no longer are. You are trying to figure out what your purpose here on earth is. There must be more than just working to make money to buy things.

WISDOM: *Direct awareness and continuity of experience give your life purpose and meaning.*

SITUATION: You have a strong image in your mind that you will only be happy when you get married, buy a house, and have children.

WISDOM: *Happiness does not come from any kind of acquisitiveness, material or psychological. Happiness comes from letting go.*

SITUATION: The last child graduated from college and moved away from home. While you are a little sad about the move, it also feels like a new beginning. After all those years of being responsible for your family, you have the urge to find a new life path. Now you just need to figure out which direction to take.

WISDOM: *Every moment and circumstance in life is an opportunity for you to experience things as they are, not as you fear or wish them to be. Every moment and circumstance has the potential for you to realize that your life is the path.*

SITUATION: As a child, daydreaming of the perfect family got you through your parents' painful and nasty divorce. Now, as an adult, daydreaming has become a habit that is creating negative consequences in your life. You spend a lot of time at it, and when your daydreams do not come true, you find that you become frustrated with life.

WISDOM: *As with many things in life, moderation is the key. Daydreaming is no exception. When you daydream too much, it takes you away from what is really happening and can lead to resentment and frustration. When you daydream in moderation and observe the effect it is having on you, it can be useful and enjoyed.*

SITUATION: It is hard to make a contribution to society in your current situation: children, husband, job, mortgage payment, car payments, saving for college, saving for retirement, medical expenses, insurance expenses . . . The list goes on. Your heart is in the right place; you just don't feel you can make a contribution to society at this time.

WISDOM: *Mothers and fathers who are calm and happy bring affection and a sense of caring into the lives of their children, thereby transforming society into something more compassionate and peaceful.*

SITUATION: Like most people, between your family and work commitments, there does not seem to be any time left over for your own hobbies. Having a hobby is important for your physical and mental well-being, but at the present time, you just can't fit it in.

WISDOM: *Acknowledge the personal expressions of culture that encircle you and are there for you to partake in. Everything, from the quilt on your bed to the design of your reading glasses, expresses the imagination and ideals of its maker. Let this inspire you to pursue your hobbies with whatever time you can eke out. Cultivate your inner life, and you will find time to be creative.*

Work

SITUATION: Responding to an email, you consider the tone of what you are about to say.

WISDOM: *Center and collect yourself each time you begin an email. Be mindful of all your words. Be conscious of your tone and whether you are saying what you really want to say.*

SITUATION: You are nervous because you are about to begin your job appraisal process. One item you need to fill out before you meet your boss is your goals for the coming year.

WISDOM: *Recognize that positive thinking is a powerful force in achieving your goals.*

SITUATION: You are writing a proposal for work. Getting the contract will have a major positive impact on your company. A lot is riding on this, and you feel the pressure.

WISDOM: *When writing something important, visualize yourself feeling very at ease about the writing. Write with confidence. You are relaxed and happy, writing smoothly and comfortably. At the end, see yourself feeling extremely pleased with what you have done and confident that you have written with quality. Keep this image in your mind as long as possible. Reinforce the visualization by repeating an affirmation like "I can handle this" or "I am very confident."*

SITUATION: You work in a busy office. It feels like you do not have time to do all the work you have to in a day. You wish you could manage work time better.

WISDOM: *If you have "no-mind," all your thinking and feeling won't get between you and the work you have to do. If you have no-mind, you lose your ego. You become your doing. You let go of your preconceptions about yourself, your life, your work—and find that your mind expands. That room is helpful for concentrating and immersing yourself in your work.*

SITUATION: The economy is going into a tailspin, and there is pressure to create more business for your company. No matter what you do, you cannot generate more business. The economy is out of your control.

WISDOM: *The world spins without your help, people do what they do, and your life will run its course one way or the other. Sometimes your plans don't work out. You can decide not to get upset, anxious, or angry about things over which you have no power. You can choose to do your job and live your life with integrity, compassion, mindful observance, and a healthy sense of humor.*

SITUATION: You had to leave work early today to go to one of your kids' school activities. You brought home work to finish up at your computer. After finishing it and turning off the computer, you feel grateful that the computer helped you. If you did not have the computer, you would not have been able to leave the office and you'd have missed your child's activity.

WISDOM: *By nodding to the computer, you recognize its contribution to your life.*

SITUATION: It was a tough day at the office, and your home has you overwhelmed. You still have more work to do after the kids go to sleep.

WISDOM: *If you are fully present in the moment, time will be suspended. That feeling of being trapped or overwhelmed will evaporate.*

SITUATION: You think that you have a great idea at work. Unfortunately, your boss does not agree that your idea is great, and you are frustrated.

WISDOM: *When you say something to someone, they may not accept it. Don't try to make them understand it intellectually. Do not argue with them; just listen to them until they find something wrong with their own objections. Try not to force your idea on them, but think about it with them.*

SITUATION: At work, you are offered a promotion—but if you accept it, you will have to relocate. You want the promotion, but you are not sure you want to move.

WISDOM: *What matters is whether you are aware of your thoughts and feelings during meditation and how you handle them. Your thoughts are just thoughts— and they are not you or reality. You are then able to step back from them and see them clearly, so you can prioritize and make sensible decisions.*

SITUATION: You overhear a professional colleague criticize you to your boss.

WISDOM: *Remember that people usually engage in negativity and excessive criticism out of feelings of jealousy, anger, or low self-esteem.*

SITUATION: At work, a controversial topic has divided the office into two groups. The boss decided to go with your plan, but he also gave you the responsibility of rebuilding office morale.

WISDOM: *Pay attention to the feelings, intentions, and thoughts beneath your words; learn to cultivate the compassion, integrity, and kindness that bring harmony to your relationships and to your mind.*

SITUATION: Your job is giving you no satisfaction, and the environment is not emotionally healthy for you. You don't know why you are afraid to seek a new job.

WISDOM: *As you look, you will see more and more clearly the patterns of habits and fears that run your life.*

SITUATION: In the midst of a recession, for the first time in your life, you find yourself laid off from work.

WISDOM: *On the shore of suffering, anger, and depression, you want to cross to the shore of well-being. Return to yourself, practice mindful breathing, look at these feelings, and smile. Doing this, you overcome pain and cross over. You can practice this every day.*

SITUATION: The company you work for is downsizing. No one knows for sure what is going to happen, but everyone has suspicions. You have been at the company for many years and are at a tricky age for seeking new employment.

WISDOM: *Brave people are intimate with fear. Fear and anxiety are always projections about something in the future. Faith means trusting the unfolding process of our lives—a willingness to let go of fears and attachments and open ourselves to the unknown in each new moment.*

SITUATION: You have two job offers, one from a big firm and one from a small firm.

WISDOM: *When you have doubts about what to do, just imagine that today is your last day. Then you will see clearly what your conscience tells you.*

SITUATION: An influential person gave you a sure-thing stock tip that you want to act on, except that the company you want to buy shares in was responsible for a major environmental accident, and they have not taken responsibility for it or helped in the cleanup.

WISDOM: *Greed, seen in the light of understanding, has less and less power to pull you into activity. You can see how much magic it takes out of the world. Every act of generosity slowly weakens the factor of greed.*

SITUATION: After retiring from a successful career, you drop off all of your work clothes at a shelter for abused women.

WISDOM: *Each day, commit a selfless act that no one else knows about.*

SITUATION: Instead of waiting for the end of the day to complete mundane projects at work, this week you are going to try to do them at the beginning of the workday.

WISDOM: *Recognize what you do with your mind, how unpresent you often are, and how delicious whatever you're doing can be—these insights make even the most mundane activities delightful and nourishing.*

SITUATION: Being in a job you can't stand is taking a heavy toll on you. You want to change everything about your job and career path.

WISDOM: *When you are aware of your intentions in the present, you can shape your future.*

SITUATION: It's Sunday morning, and you are already dreading Monday morning at work.

WISDOM: *The first step is to stop, notice, and appreciate what is happening. Even if this is all we do, it's revolutionary.*

SITUATION: Your boss was mean-spirited, unfriendly, and incompetent at work. He was the worst boss you ever had and created the most negative work environment you had ever been in. He lost his job, and now you've been promoted to take his place. You know that you will not make the same mistakes he did.

WISDOM: *Inwardly thank one who disturbs or harms you—for such kind teachings. Now you know you must avoid creating any further causes for such effects. Those who harm you are like teachers showing you the effects of your actions.*

SITUATION: A new co-worker is taking the office by storm, but you get the feeling he is superficially charming and more concerned about his own success than the office's.

WISDOM: *See the false as false, the true as true.*

SITUATION: Sometimes it gets really slow at work, and there is not enough to do, so you pretend to be busy. In reality, you are just wasting time and energy.

WISDOM: *It is a cardinal sin to waste time. To waste time is to squander the here and now, which, if you think about it, is all you have.*

SITUATION: The creative well has run dry. No matter how hard you try to concentrate, you cannot come up with the creative solutions you once could at work.

WISDOM: *It is very important to have a center. Without a center you can do routine things, but you will never be creative. Centering allows you to live at the maximum, at the peak.*

SITUATION: The stress from work has gotten to you. You feel tired, have no energy, are not breathing properly, have gained weight—you even notice that your hairline has changed since you took this new position.

WISDOM: *When you let stress get to you, everything is bad, unmanageable, more dramatic, and out of control. When you get enough sleep, exercise, healthy food, meditation, and try to approach life with a positive attitude, things seem a lot easier.*

SITUATION: At work, you are part of a team that designed a new product. When it is demonstrated to co-workers, it gets panned on several levels. You and your team try to defend the product's design.

WISDOM: *You believe that it is difficult to let go, but in truth it is much more difficult and painful to hold and protect. Anything you grasp ahold of is surrounded by fear and defensiveness.*

SITUATION: Your boss intimidates you to begin with. Now you find yourself having to give her bad news about a project you have been working on. You're afraid that you will freeze up when you talk to her.

WISDOM: *Try being aware of the other person as a stressor without losing balance of mind. Ground yourself in breathing and see the situation as a whole without reacting out of fear.*

SITUATION: You are sitting at the computer with your résumé on the screen, laid off from your job because of the economy. You just don't know if you have the strength to update it and go on job interviews again.

WISDOM: *With ordinary talent and extraordinary perseverance, all things are attainable.*

SITUATION: You didn't realize that your first job out of college was going to be so unexciting and boring. You thought that you were going to be involved in million-dollar deals right off the bat.

WISDOM: *Unrealistic expectations tarnish your appreciation of life, weighing down the buoyancy of the present moment.*

SITUATION: You dress the part and live the lifestyle of success. You think you have an important job because you make a lot of money and have a lot of people working for you, but there is something missing. You don't know what it is, but you are not as happy as you should be.

WISDOM: *Letting go of self a little improves life. Letting go of self a lot brings happiness and joy.*

SITUATION: A co-worker recently criticized you in a meeting. Now, at the next meeting, it is your turn to speak about some of the shortfalls of her department.

WISDOM: *Even if someone criticizes you, speak of that person with kindness. Reply with kindness and compassion to negativity and harm.*

SITUATION: It is never an easy task, but you have to fire someone at work because they have taken too many sick days. It is eating at you, and it's going to be difficult to let this well-liked employee go, but the company has strict absenteeism rules that must be followed.

WISDOM: *Firing an employee can have as big an impact on yourself as it does on the person you let go. There is no one right way to fire someone, but there are some very wrong ways to do it. Try to do it in a respectful way so that you do not feel awful about yourself, too.*

SITUATION: You have the choice of working in a private industry and making a lot of money or in a non-profit business that helps people but would mean a lot less money.

WISDOM: *The Buddha said it is a great fortune to have an occupation that allows us to be happy, to help others, and to generate compassion and understanding in this world.*

SITUATION: Business meals are difficult for you because you are trying to eat more mindfully. It seems that when you eat a meal out with colleagues or clients on an expense account, everyone tends to go a little overboard.

WISDOM: *If you eat with others who are not eating mindfully, you can stop every once in a while and look around, breathe, and smile.*

SITUATION: Colleagues invited you to go out after work. You made an excuse that you were not feeling well and could not go. Unfortunately, you then went out to the same place where the work party ended up, and you got caught in a lie.

WISDOM: *If you get caught in a lie, it will be assumed that it is not the first lie that you told.*

SITUATION: You are a young lawyer, and it has not taken you long to see and understand that our prisons are filled with mostly poor and minority people. This is really bothering you.

WISDOM: *Become aware of the suffering caused by exploitation, social injustice, and oppression. Commit yourself to cultivating loving kindness and learning ways to work for the well-being of people, animals, and plants. Commit to practicing generosity by sharing your time, energy, and material resources with those who are in real need.*

SITUATION: In your place of work, it was revealed through the grapevine that, on average, male employees make more money than the women for the same positions.

WISDOM: *The difference between men and women is only gender. Their ability to achieve wisdom and happiness is the same.*

SITUATION: Two co-workers are in an argument, and you are in the middle. You see both sides, and you want the argument to end before it gets ugly and uncomfortable.

WISDOM: *Act to promote harmony and unity. Refrain from allowing your attachments and expectations to cause or further an argument.*

SITUATION: One of your co-workers is so competitive at work that you are becoming dissatisfied with your job. You don't believe everything should be a competition.

WISDOM: *Temper your natural reaction to a difficult or competitive co-worker and show compassion toward him because his personal situation is influencing his motivation.*

SITUATION: You are a manager of a department that just produced an unbelievably successful quarter. You are happy for yourself and your team.

WISDOM: *Take a moment to appreciate what you have done each day by being mindful in your work. Consider how you can build on that the next day.*

SITUATION: Your job is so boring it is really beginning to negatively affect your entire life.

WISDOM: *Never continue in a career or job you don't enjoy. If you're happy in what you're doing, you'll like yourself, and you'll have inner peace. If you have that, along with physical health, you have more success than you could possibly have imagined.*

SITUATION: After a successful career, you have decided to retire. Yet you feel that you still have a lot left in the tank, and you want to continue working at something worthwhile. While this idea is exciting, it is also a little scary.

WISDOM: *Your work is to discover your work and then, with all your heart, to give yourself to it. The Buddha said it is a great fortune to have an occupation that allows us to be happy, to help others, and to generate compassion and understanding in this world.*

SITUATION: After a lot of hard work on a project, the plans are rejected. The small company you own has one more chance to satisfy the client. The entire office is now suffering from low self-esteem because of the previous rejection.

WISDOM: *One way to foster self-esteem is by creating a balanced workplace. Move on from this particular situation and look for ways to make the workplace and the job more enjoyable and fulfilling.*

SITUATION: You have a great idea at work. You try to contribute it in a meeting, but everyone is focused on another problem and ignores your idea. You want to bring it up again, but you are not sure how or when.

WISDOM: *There is no need to worry that a good idea or the solution to a problem will be lost. What is of value will be available at the proper moment.*

SITUATION: There is a job posting at work that would be a great promotion for you. Many others see it in the same way and have also applied for the position. It seems everyone is getting caught up in who will get the promotion.

WISDOM: *Do your own useful work without regard to the honor or admiration your efforts might win from others.*

SITUATION: You are new to the company you work for. You've noticed an unusual and pleasant custom. The president of the company has lunch at least once a month with the mailroom and maintenance workers.

WISDOM: *A person's happiness and success in life depend not so much upon what he has or upon what position he occupies, as upon what he is and the heart he carries into his position.*

SITUATION: The big promotion is everything you thought it would be. After years of hard work, you feel that you are finally rewarded with the big title and salary you deserve.

WISDOM: *It is neither wealth nor splendor, but tranquility and occupation that give happiness.*

SITUATION: Your place of work is rife with people gossiping and circulating rumors. While you do not feel comfortable with rumors, sometimes you get caught up in them and repeat them.

WISDOM: *You can never really take your words back, so it is critical that you develop such mindfulness about your speech that you do not start rumors or gossip in the first place.*

SITUATION: Not only do you enjoy your job, you also enjoy most of the people you work with. Like every workplace, some days are difficult. But for the most part, you are friends with the people you work with.

WISDOM: *Be friendly to the people around you at work. Being kind makes things uncomplicated. It creates an environment that benefits everyone. You can practice this anytime, anywhere, with anyone.*

SITUATION: You have made great strides in getting your personal life going in the right direction. You want to take the next step and get your work life in order by making your workday worthwhile.

WISDOM: *Take a moment to appreciate what you have done each day, being mindful in your work. Consider how you can build on that the next day.*

SITUATION: As it is for most people these days, it is difficult for you to balance work and a personal life. It seems that you spend so much time and energy at work that there is not much left over for anything else.

WISDOM: *Cultivating balance in your life can help you get in touch with your inner self. Every day, think a little, feel a little, move a little, rest a little, eat a little, drink a little, sleep a little, work a little, and meditate a little. If you don't let any one activity dominate, you will cultivate an inner equilibrium and contentment.*

SITUATION: As you move up the ranks in your office, you make a vow to yourself that you want to be an effective leader—not just a yes-person, but someone who makes a difference to both customers and employees.

WISDOM: *What you do not like as a follower, do not do as a leader. Be an effective leader by seeking good ideas from all levels. Be present, focused, less reactive, and listen deeply.*

SITUATION: Your job is a big part of your life, and you have a new, demanding boss. You are feeling so frustrated with work right now that the negative emotions are spilling over into your personal life. You feel incompetent because of the way your boss is treating you.

WISDOM: *It may not seem like it at the time, but the root of your suffering is found internally. It comes from the limitations you have placed on yourself, not from a demanding boss, who can have no negative effect on you unless you allow it. The boss is suffering, so show her compassion in her suffering.*

SITUATION: On your most recent job review, your boss made a comment about how you need to cultivate good working relationships with your employees.

WISDOM: *More often than not, what you say and how you say it determines the quality of you relationships. When you don't say the positive things that need to be said, when you unconsciously say hurtful or meaningless things, and when you fail to address problems in your relationships directly and lovingly, suffering arises.*

SITUATION: You were recently given the duty of training a new employee in the office. It is going to be difficult to fit in the training along with all your other responsibilities.

WISDOM: *Think of the impact of a happy, loving, and compassionate teacher on a student.*

SITUATION: With the economy faltering and pressure on at work, you are noticing that most of the people in the office are whining and acting in a negative manner. It is becoming like a cancer and spreading to just about every person in the office.

WISDOM: *Resistance, moping, complaining, and whining are insidious and self-destructive. Negativity takes its toll, unbalancing your life.*

SITUATION: For the most part, you enjoy your job and the company you work for. But sometimes the elderly customers you work with try your patience. You hope you give them the service they require to help them out.

WISDOM: *Before starting work for the day, take a moment to reflect. Acknowledge the value of your job. Offer gratitude for the opportunity to contribute something of value. Ask for the skills and qualities you will need to perform the duties to the best of your ability.*

SITUATION: Every time a new program is installed on your computer, your frustration level rises because the process has never gone smoothly.

WISDOM: *When an unpleasant state like frustration cannot draw you out, you are on the road to freedom and happiness.*

SITUATION: Gas prices have increased tremendously, and inflation has emerged as an economic reality. Your boss has asked everyone to come up with ideas to help the company save money and benefit the employees, too. Your idea is to let some workers telecommute. It will save on office space for the company and driving expenses for employees.

WISDOM: *Regularly ask how we can simplify, use less, and share more. Earth has only a certain amount of resources to go around. Conserving them benefits the entire world.*

SITUATION: You are in charge of a long meeting at work. You are working very hard to make sure it runs efficiently and effectively. Co-workers are giving up a lot of working time to attend this meeting.

WISDOM: *When a meeting is scheduled to last a long time, besides being well prepared and organized for it, take periodic breathing breaks. Stop the meeting and have everyone take a few deep breaths to bring them back to focus.*

SITUATION: There has been some turnover at work lately, and you are not sure why. It seems that the people you hire either do not work out for you or, if they seem to be working out, they leave after a few months. It is starting to be a drain on the company. You have devoted a lot of resources to making sure you hire the right people.

WISDOM: *It is impossible to be absolutely right all the time. Happiness comes when your work and words benefit both yourself and others. Keep trying. If you plant peaches, you will get peaches. Karma works this way.*

SITUATION: You are currently working for a company in an industry that is dying. There are few opportunities for growth. You did not plan on staying at this job for long, but one thing led to another, and before you knew it, ten years had gone by. You do not want another ten years to pass before you work on your career development.

WISDOM: *Before you devise a plan to develop your career and work life, it helps to have your spiritual life in order. Remember the idea of right livelihood when pursuing your career and work life: work, earn money, and spend money in a way that causes no harm. Consciously choose work that helps people, don't be greedy, and practice careful consumption.*

SITUATION: Sexual harassment at work is beginning to cross a line you are uncomfortable with and causes you pain and suffering. Working in a mainly male industry, you expected some things to come up in conversations and actions, but now they are going a little too far, and you have spoken up about it. You do not want to name names so people could lose their jobs, but you want the harassment to stop.

WISDOM: *Why cling to the pain and the wrongs of yesterday? Why hold on to the very things that keep you from hope and love? The pain is inevitable, but suffering is optional.*

SITUATION: Part of your work responsibility is to mediate between squabbling co-workers. In a particularly challenging case, it appears that one side has a better point than the other. It is your job to be fair.

WISDOM: *People tend to reassure themselves by blaming others, and they find comfort in believing their suffering is caused by incompetent and selfish organizations and leaders. In the workplace, this loss of perspective can be harmful, leading to arguments and conflicts. Distancing yourself from the content of thought allows you to regain a sense of objectivity and freedom so you can permit the essence of thought to massage the mind and come up with solutions.*

SITUATION: There was a merger at your firm recently. Now that the dust has settled, the real work begins. One of the first tasks of the new company is to reduce staff. Unfortunately, part of this responsibility falls on you. While you are happy to still have your job, it is painful to let other people go.

WISDOM: *Compassion is not the same as pity. Pity is the feeling you have for the homeless man begging. Compassion is understanding that all of us are in this situation together. Genuine compassion is based on the recognition that others have the right to happiness just like yourself.*

SITUATION: A clique is developing at work, and you are not comfortable with it. Some of the people in the group are your friends, but when they get together after work, it can turn pretty ugly. There is a lot of gossiping and backstabbing.

WISDOM: *When the mind is soft and non-grasping, you won't get caught in the melodramas that cause pain to you and others.*

SITUATION: You are dealing with a bully at work. This person calls you an epithet that hurts your feelings. In meetings, he is mean and belittling to you. The job you once loved has turned into a nightmare. It feels like high school all over again.

WISDOM: *A bully is someone who is so unhappy with himself that he takes his sadness and anger out on others. Bullies always use wrong speech.*

SITUATION: The alarm didn't go off, so you start the day running late. You spill coffee on your blouse and have to take time changing. Traffic is heavy, so you are even later for work. The boss is in the office conducting a meeting, which, of course, you are late to. When you finally sit down at your desk, it is piled up with messages for you to return.

WISDOM: *When you are having a bad day, stop and take a moment to think: What makes a bad day bad? Why have I labeled this day a bad day? What can I do to make a bad day into a good one?*

SITUATION: Someone at work is selling counterfeit watches and purses. They are keeping it low-key, but you are aware that it is going on.

WISDOM: *Does it really matter whether someone else is innocent or guilty? Only worry about yourself and your own actions.*

SITUATION: You really do not like your job. You know that you are in the wrong career field. You really want to be a teacher, and you know that you would be good at it. But you are afraid to make the move.

WISDOM: *In work, do what you enjoy. When the work and the worker are one, none of the other stuff matters.*

SITUATION: You are getting ready for an important job interview. You are both nervous and excited about it.

WISDOM: *Before a job interview, visualize yourself walking in and exuding self-confidence. The exchange between you is positive, and the interviewer looks enthusiastic when you are speaking. At the end, the interviewer shows a lot of enthusiasm for what you have said, and you feel happy that your performance has been so impressive. Keep this image in your mind as long as possible. Reinforce the visualization by repeating an affirmation like "I can handle this" or "I am very confident."*

SITUATION: You are accepting bids for a project at work. One of the companies that is making a bid offers you a subtle bribe to give them inside information for an unfair advantage.

WISDOM: *The Buddha's words are pointers in the right direction. You have to change your own heart and mind. If at any time something doesn't feel right to you, why not honor your feelings? An attitude of trusting in yourself and your own basic goodness is important. You can see how comfortable, relaxed, free, and peaceful you feel when you act ethically.*

SITUATION: You are getting mixed messages from your boss at work. Some days she seems very friendly toward you, and other days she seems to not like you at all. It is having an impact on your work and emotions. You want to like your boss, but she is making it tough.

WISDOM: *Tame your mind so that you may bring peace and well-being into your heart and the hearts of all beings.*

SITUATION: A co-worker has very few friends because she is so serious all the time. Many people at work make fun of her because of her disposition. She never laughs in the office, and you get the impression that she is not happy outside of work either. You find it difficult to spend time with her because her seriousness brings you down.

WISDOM: *There is a common fundamental need that all people in the world share: a desire for happiness. When you live your life with this in mind, you become mutually supportive and help to lessen suffering.*

SITUATION: A co-worker and friend recently got promoted and now has more power than you do in the office. You are happy for your friend, but you have noticed some changes in her personality since the promotion. It seems like she is focusing more on satisfying her own needs and less on the needs of her underlings. She is also acting like the rules everyone else is expected to follow do not apply to her. It has become difficult for you to be around her.

WISDOM: *To avoid the pitfalls of power, seek a mentor or confidant who will not be afraid to tell you when you are behaving insensitively toward others. Make sure you choose someone who will be totally honest with you. Power is no good if you lose everything else.*

SITUATION: You want to get back at a person who has been bossing and bullying you around at work for years. You've found something out about them that will just about destroy their career. You can taste how good it will feel to finally take this person down.

WISDOM: *In destroying your enemy, you destroy yourself as well.*

SITUATION: You have a client at work who never calls you back when she says she will. She knows that she is an important client to you, and you have to put aside a good amount of time to deal with her business. When she does not call back at the appointed time, it messes up your day and your responsibilities to your other clients.

WISDOM: *Compassion allows you to transform resentment into forgiveness and fear into respect.*

SITUATION: Out of respect to others, you try to respond to email messages within 24 hours of receiving them. Even if someone is asking you a question for which you have no answer, you reply that you have to do research and will get back to them. It is frustrating to you when you email someone and they do not reply in a timely manner.

WISDOM: *Your suffering is generated from within your own mind. Fixed opinions make you feel self-defensive and anxious; cravings make you feel frustrated and dissatisfied.*

SITUATION: A co-worker's habit of lying is so great that you get the feeling they actually believe the lies they are telling. It has become a joke at work, because no one believes anything this person says anymore.

WISDOM: *You should never knowingly speak a lie, for your advantage, someone else's, or any reason whatsoever. Telling lies arises from an inability or unwillingness to see the situation as it is, to speak and listen genuinely from the heart. To actively practice not lying to yourself is liberating. To not lie to others liberates them as well.*

SITUATION: One of your worst fears come true: you lose your job. As the news gets around to family and friends, you try to spin the situation so you do not feel like a pathetic loser. You know you lost your job because of the poor economy, but it is hard to convince other people of this.

WISDOM: *In times of fear and struggle, you can exhibit tremendous strength and become resourceful beyond your imagination. While the unknown can be absolutely terrifying to walk into, it can also be exciting and offer many wonderful opportunities.*

SITUATION: You have been doing the same job for more than 15 years. The boredom is really starting to get to you. Your mind feels like it is asleep. There are no new challenges in your work.

WISDOM: *Maintaining inspiration in the day-to-day duties of work requires you to approach your job as you do play. The same hobby can be exciting for many years. Viewing your work the same way helps keep your imagination fresh.*

SITUATION: Your boss at work is abusive to her subordinates. She does not care how she affects others. You have never seen anything like this before.

WISDOM: *In a working environment, if you are being abused by a boss, you do not have to be passive about it. You should do what you can to stop it and should not be afraid to protect yourself.*

SITUATION: It is St. Patrick's Day, and you have to be at work because you have used up all your vacation time. Your friends have taken the day off and are having a great time partying. You know this because they keep calling you as they go from place to place celebrating the day. You really don't want to be at work.

WISDOM: *Mental suffering results from a desire to be in a state other than the state we're in, wishing we were elsewhere.*

SITUATION: You missed your child's school play because a meeting at work went longer than you had anticipated. Everyone in your family feels like you let them down—and so do you. It is difficult to be torn between work and family.

WISDOM: *Contemplate the positive qualities of an experience, even a bad one, and refrain from saying or doing anything that might cause further damage or escalate anger.*

SITUATION: Your favorite boss recently retired. He was the perfect boss for you. The new boss does not possess the same qualities as your old boss. Although you want to give the new boss a fair chance, you know it will not be the same as before.

WISDOM: *No longer distracted by coming attractions, you will stop missing the main feature.*

SITUATION: You thought for sure that you were going to get the job you applied for. The interviewer said you were qualified and just the type of person the company was looking for. After anxiously waiting for the phone call with an offer, you were surprised when they finally called and said you did not get the position. Your mood went from happy to deeply sad.

WISDOM: *When thoughts of pain and hurt begin to overwhelm you, sit and make yourself smile. Just sit and physically and mentally make yourself smile. You may even be surprised and produce a good laugh.*

SITUATION: Your last several job interviews have not gone well. You realize that the economy is very tough and there is a lot of competition for jobs. You are doing everything you can to prepare yourself for your next interview. You are even trying to psyche yourself up by talking to yourself.

WISDOM: *Life doesn't promise anything. More important, every experience can teach you something. Opening yourself to the positive possibilities inherent in every experience is the way to grow.*

SITUATION: You heard about a job opening at your company that you really want. It has not been officially announced yet, but you want to put your name in the running right away. You know that you are the perfect person for the position. You are going to tell your boss that you are interested in it.

WISDOM: *Remember, as soon as you get the object or experience you have been longing for, you move on to another desire. The more you pursue pleasure, the more desire you experience. Don't think you're entitled or insist that the world adapt to your tastes and desires. Make your effort, try your best, then let go.*

SITUATION: You read in your alumni magazine that one of your best friends in college got a huge promotion at work. She is now much higher than you are on the corporate ladder. While this is a wonderful opportunity for your friend, you are having trouble feeling happy for her.

WISDOM: *It is part of human nature to tend to yourself and your day-to-day needs. It is natural to protect yourself and try to achieve happiness. But this causes the mind to think in only terms of "me"—a major obstacle to achieving happiness. Try to change your focus by including others in your wish for happiness.*

SITUATION: The economy is going to hell in a handbasket. The manufacturing company you work for is feeling the effects of the economy going south. There is real concern that many manufacturing jobs are going to be outsourced to a foreign country to save money. You don't know how the problem can be solved another way.

WISDOM: *If you cannot solve a problem, then what is the use of worrying about it?*

SITUATION: At an office meeting, your boss asks you a question that she apparently thinks you should know the answer to—but you don't. You feel embarrassed and unworthy, but you admit that you do not know the answer and will do some research on it. This is not good enough for the boss, who asks someone else if they know the answer—and they do.

WISDOM: *To find the truth, one must first be truthful to oneself. Take what you have learned from this experience and build something positive with it. Try harder, show that you care.*

SITUATION: You went to college to become a teacher. Unfortunately, when you began to teach in the classroom, you realized that you did not enjoy it at all and you were not a very effective teacher. Now you feel like you failed, even though it seemed like a ton of bricks were lifted off your chest when you handed in your resignation.

WISDOM: *A way to deal with life's failures and disappointments is to move deeper into life and devote energy to figuring it out, not turning away from it.*

SITUATION: At work, you have a reputation as a no-nonsense type of person. Your career has always been important to you, and you work hard at it. Now that you are moving up the corporate ladder, your mentor advises you that to be a more effective manager, you need to develop your small-talk skills, which are important for you as a manager in terms of communicating effectively with your subordinates.

WISDOM: *It helps to stay in the present moment and speak with compassion when talking to someone. This way, you are better able to manage your own thoughts and impulses as well as to contend with the thoughts and impulses of the person you are talking to.*

SITUATION: Every job review you have ever had says the same thing: you need to become more assertive and apply yourself more. No matter how hard you try, it just does not seem to come across to other people.

WISDOM: *An aspect of being mindful is the ability to apply yourself. Applying yourself tests your limits. Never be fearful of applying yourself, because you never know what good may come out of it.*

SITUATION: Morale at work has sunk to an all-time low because of merger and acquisition talk. Not only is everyone in your department worried about keeping their jobs, they are also worried about how things will change once the merger goes through. The company, and your department, needs a morale booster.

WISDOM: *Meditate or simply look at the open sky. Focus on anything that encourages you to stay on the brink and not solidify into a view.*

SITUATION: Once a month, a group of your colleagues gets together for a few drinks after work. Every time, the conversation ends up becoming a gripe session. Everyone complains about their work, the boss, and the company. Although some of the complaints are funny, you would love to be in an environment that did not focus on griping so much.

WISDOM: *Try not to complain, especially about things that are not likely to change. Even complaints tempered with humor do not serve any purpose. Try to alleviate problems with actions, not complaints.*

SITUATION: This is your first job out of college. Although you are young, you are enthusiastic and ready to show your stuff. After your training period, you are given your first project to manage. You are responsible for a team of ten employees to make sure a contract for another company is administered properly.

WISDOM: *Besides being fair in wages, benefits, and treatment, an effective boss also understands the strengths of her employees. When you assign tasks according to employees' strengths, you create a pleasant and productive environment in which to work. Everyone wins.*

SITUATION: As you walk from your office desk to the conference room, the only thing you can think of is how boring this all-day meeting about sexual harassment set up by Human Resources is going to be. They could address the situation in an hour, but no, they have to drag it out all day long. You cannot think of anything more boring.

WISDOM: *Feeling bored is one of those tricky emotions we humans experience. The real question is not whether you are bored, but whether you are boring. The answer is, if you feel bored, it's you who are boring. Life is so exciting, even in its most mundane phases, that it can never be boring. When you feel bored, you drain the life out of the moment. Every moment is important and should be cherished, not wasted.*

SITUATION: You were in your dream job. You loved your work, your bosses, your co-workers, and your company. You looked forward to Monday mornings instead of dreading them. Then came the merger, which changed everything. New responsibilities, new bosses, new co-workers, and a new company. Your dream job has become a nightmare. Work is no longer enjoyable or satisfying.

WISDOM: *Change is often different than you imagine, and it can cause you to feel hurt, sad, angry, helpless, or defeated. Yet everything changes in constant transformation. Nothing is permanent, and nothing you do is permanent. Even impermanence is impermanent.*

SITUATION: At work, someone plays a practical joke on you that, while it may be funny, undermines your authority and leaves you embarrassed. Not knowing who did this to you, it is difficult for you to look at the people you work with. Your boss thinks the joke was hysterical, so you can't go to her for help.

WISDOM: *No one outside yourself can rule you inside.*

SITUATION: By nature, you have a tendency to be impatient. The job market is tight because of a down economy. You have a secure, decent job with good pay, but you are not happy in this position. It is difficult for you to be patient and not jump the gun looking for a new job during this tight job market. You have financial obligations and should be patient until the economy improves.

WISDOM: *When you feel impatient with your work, realize that you are resisting the way things are.*

SITUATION: One of your friends invited you to come to a World Series baseball game. Your favorite team is playing, and you have never been to a World Series game before. Unfortunately, the game is during the work week, and you are out of vacation time. You decide to call in sick even though you are not.

WISDOM: *You will suffer in this life and the next from both the actions and the knowledge of things you do wrong. If you do good, you can achieve overwhelming happiness in this world, which will also be with you in the next.*

SITUATION: A message came down from management today informing all employees that they are no longer allowed to make personal phone calls or write personal emails at work. During this difficult economic period, the company needs to be as efficient as possible, and personal phone calls or emails could get you fired. This comes as a shock to the employees, because no one realized this privilege was being abused.

WISDOM: *Work with mindful awareness toward inner and outer harmony so that you may live peacefully and help generate accord among others. If you can accept this business decision, you will eventually let any upset go and be fine.*

SITUATION: At the office, your boss planned an outing for a small group of employees. To pay for it, she told you to fill out an expense account making up charges to cover the costs.

WISDOM: *In both large matters and small details, remain true to your deepest principles so that your integrity can be a gift to others.*

SITUATION: At your new job, you are shocked by how well the other employees multitask. In the past, you have always tried to do one thing and do that well. It scares you to have to learn the new skill of multitasking.

WISDOM: *Recognize your work as an opportunity to extend your spiritual practice, even as you are fulfilling your obligations.*

SITUATION: After a difficult day at work, you like to be left alone in privacy. Taking a warm bath helps. Unfortunately, your spouse thinks you need to talk to him about your day to help you feel better. The polarization of needs and desires usually ends up causing a fight and making things worse.

WISDOM: *You experience aversion whenever you reject something because you deem it unpleasant. But aversion throws you farther off balance and makes it impossible to find peace. Recognize the destructiveness of aversion. Let go of it each time it arises, and take advantage of the opportunity it gives you for insight, wisdom, and spiritual growth.*

SITUATION: You own a small landscaping business. Unfortunately, over the weekend you broke your leg playing softball. You will not be able to operate the equipment you need to for your business. After years of hard work, you do not want to see your business crumble because of this injury. You are in crisis mode.

WISDOM: *Situations can elicit fear and anxiety. But these are projections about a future that has not yet happened. When fear arises, separate yourself from the source of the fear. Hold your fear gently, with compassion for yourself, so that the actuality of the present moment banishes it. Fear is impermanent and will pass away.*

SITUATION: The workday grind is beginning to get to you. It seems like all you do is wake up, go to work, come home, and go to bed. You need a little pick-me-up to wipe away the blues.

WISDOM: *Whenever you are experiencing strong desire, anxiety, or even fear, you are not in the present moment. You are longing for something to be different. Instead, infuse your life with mindful attention in each moment so that you may live with love, happiness, and choices that are wise and contribute to genuine happiness.*

SITUATION: You cannot wait to retire. After working your entire adult life, you are so ready to retire that you can barely stand it. No more getting up early to get to work on time, no more answering to incompetent bosses, no more worrying about job security. Your own time is coming.

WISDOM: *Take joy in your own achievements. Value yourself and appreciate what you have attained. Cultivate gratitude for all the blessings in your life and also delight in others' successes.*

SITUATION: At work, you are going to miss a deadline on a team project because you are sick. You try to get the work done, but the flu has just wiped you out. Not only do you feel ill, you feel bad about missing the deadline because it is holding up the rest of team from progressing on their part of the project. This delay is costing the company a lot of money.

WISDOM: *If you've been a good worker, have faith. If you've put in an honest day's work at all times except during this illness, you have done your best. Be forthright and approach the situation with dignity.*

SITUATION: The industry you work in is going through tough times. You are in your early fifties and do not want to retire, nor can you afford to. Your company has offered you a job-buyout package, so you decide to go back to school to become a teacher. You are excited about the change of occupations and the new work adventure that is in front of you.

WISDOM: *Nothing contributes so much to tranquilizing the mind as a steady purpose.*

SITUATION: Your hair just will not cooperate today. No matter what you try, it does not do what you want it to. You have an important business meeting, and you want to look your best when you deliver your presentation. But your bad hair day is not helping your confidence.

WISDOM: *You just gotta laugh at the insignificance of one hairdo among six billion hairdos. Think of flowers that are beautiful with no effort. You are beautiful, too, no matter what your hair is doing. Laugh at it, because humor is healing and connects you to others, who also experience these things.*

SITUATION: This year, the candles on your birthday cake can heat a good-sized room.

WISDOM: *Enjoy and appreciate growing old, instead of dreading it.*

School

SITUATION: Your child has been having difficulty with tests at school. The more he meets failure, the less he is inclined to study. You are trying to break this habit and teach him how to study better.

WISDOM: *If there is preparation, there will be no regret.*

SITUATION: For career day at school, your child volunteers you to speak.

WISDOM: *Imagine that all your comments and opinions are like drops of water falling into a pond and that the ripples represent the signals you send out to those around you.*

SITUATION: Your child's third-grade class takes a field trip to an assisted living complex to help plant a garden, and you are a chaperone. Being relatively young, with healthy parents, you've never given much thought to growing old. But after seeing the condition of some of the elderly people in this facility, you change your perspective quickly. The fear of growing old is now real to you. You cannot imagine living life in the condition that some of these people are in.

WISDOM: *The fear of dying is a powerful emotion experienced by most people. But, when we recognize this fear and accept it, we feel better and are able to live peacefully with the reality of old age, sickness, and death.*

SITUATION: Math is not your strongest subject, but you are the family tutor tonight with your child's homework. No matter how many different ways you explain it, she is just not getting it. You are becoming frustrated.

WISDOM: *When you find yourself frustrated with yourself or another, remember that at this very moment you are invited to soften your resistance and open your heart.*

SITUATION: While correcting your child's school report, you feel that the work is not up to his ability.

WISDOM: *Aim to be constructive, positive, and empathetic. Give support and encouragement. Be open and sensitive to what others are experiencing and you will truly see and hear them.*

SITUATION: Teachers' salaries keep going up, and your taxes keep going up to pay for these raises, yet your children are losing out because the Board of Education is cutting corners at the schools by eliminating programs such as music and art classes and after-school activities. Classroom size has increased, and parents are charged for their children participating in athletics. It does not seem fair that the students, who are the most innocent, get hurt the most.

WISDOM: *Be mindfully present for life's precious moments with openness and gratitude so that the whole world can be your teacher.*

SITUATION: At a Board of Education meeting you are attending, you are scheduled to give a speech about a program you believe in that is being terminated because of budget cuts. You feel that the children in the school district will be harmed and lose an important activity for their growth because of this cut.

WISDOM: *In finding the willingness to pause and listen to yourself before you speak, you may discover the confidence and calmness to speak with firmness and clarity.*

SITUATION: At your daughter's school they do an annual charity fundraiser that you love to chaperone—an all-night walkathon. There is just something about this event that you look forward to each year.

WISDOM: *Doing good deeds helps you enter into a world of joy. When awareness and charity are high, so is happiness.*

SITUATION: You have been taking dance lessons for a long time, and you are confident in your dancing ability. At the auditions for the school musical, you do very well and get a lead part.

WISDOM: *People with integrity and confidence do not need to shout; their silence speaks as loud as their words.*

SITUATION: During your high school election, you lose the race for the presidency by a few votes to someone who, admittedly, is more popular than you are. It hurts to think that the election was based on popularity, not substance.

WISDOM: *Turn a major loss, fall, or setback in life into an awakening opportunity or moment.*

SITUATION: You are a top student at your school, but you are struggling with an advanced math course. You are embarrassed to ask for help from the teacher, because then you would be admitting that you have a weakness in this subject, and people would not think of you as being so smart.

WISDOM: *Give endlessly, fail repeatedly, see the weaknesses in yourself on a daily basis, fail and fail again . . . but then get up and try again.*

SITUATION: A debate is raging in your town about teaching sex education in the middle school. The arguments both for and against it make sense to you.

WISDOM: *A little reflection tells you that spoken and written words can have enormous consequences for good and harm. Words can break lives, create enemies, and start wars. Words can also give wisdom, heal divisions, and create peace.*

SITUATION: You go to pick up your high school–aged son after school because his car is in the shop being repaired. While waiting in the parking lot on this beautiful spring day, you notice that the girls are wearing some pretty revealing outfits. Girls did not dress like this when you were in high school. You consider yourself reasonably liberal and modern, but you have to admit that their outfits leave you a little concerned.

WISDOM: *A moment of recognition about a judgmental mind is a moment of freedom and wisdom.*

SITUATION: During your last final exam at school, you have to cheat to get an answer correct. You don't get caught, and you do well on the exam, but you do feel guilty that you cheated on that one question.

WISDOM: *When you are aware that you are caught by a problem, you are already freeing yourself. Any moment can enlighten you if you see its totality, its complexities, its simpleness. Rediscover the power of self-forgiveness.*

SITUATION: During class, the teacher catches you talking to the person sitting next to you. This is not the first time it has happened, and the teacher is beginning to get angry about it.

WISDOM: *To talk a lot unnecessarily is like allowing thousands of weeds to grow in a garden. It would be better to have a flower.*

SITUATION: In your small town, the school honor roll is listed in the newspaper. This semester you did not make honors because of some things happening in your personal life. You know that everyone reads the honor roll, and you feel bad that you did not make it.

WISDOM: *Making mistakes in life should not lead you to feeling inferior to others. Try not to feel unworthy. Awaken, appreciate the joy life can bring, and continue on a path of freedom.*

SITUATION: A new student in school has very bad breath. You are hearing all kinds of negative comments about this new student because of it. You know how these things can fester.

WISDOM: *Wise speech is a careful blend of cultivation and restraint. Cultivate speech that is truthful, helpful, kind, and leads to harmony or healing. Restrain yourself from words of harshness, divisiveness, and dishonesty.*

SITUATION: Just before your senior class picture is to be taken, you have a face breakout. You kind of freak out and become upset while waiting in line for your photo.

WISDOM: *You can learn how to be calm by paying attention to your breath, and you can learn that there are many benefits to being calm.*

SITUATION: You are an artist and musician, not an athlete. In gym class, the most dreaded day for you is the day you have to take the physical fitness test. It is embarrassing and humiliating to have to try to perform in front of your peers when you know you can never pass the test.

WISDOM: *Stop comparing yourself and setting yourself up for unhappiness. You risk feeling superior or inferior, as any type of comparison separates you from others. Instead, identify with others. Experience interconnectedness.*

SITUATION: At your school newspaper, the administration is putting the kibosh on a truthful but unfavorable story you wrote about a faculty member. The student body gets wind of the situation and is intent on fighting this kind of censorship. Things are quickly spinning out of control.

WISDOM: *A voice rooted in wisdom treasures truthfulness, respect, and compassion. Although there is great elaboration of right speech in Buddhist texts, it all condenses into two general principles. Is it true? Is it useful? Practicing these principles fosters increased sensitivity.*

SITUATION: Your child is going through the college application process. He has an aptitude for science and engineering, and he is also a talented artist. Considering the high cost of college and the realities of the job market, you are trying to control his decision making by encouraging him to pursue schools with science and engineering programs so he will be able to find a good job upon graduation. However, he wants to go to art school.

WISDOM: *Thinking gives you a sense of control. If you think, think, think, you'll have control, right? Not really. No one controls who you are inside and what you choose to do. In the same way, you don't control who anyone else is or what anyone else does. Since you don't really have control over people and the world, go along for the ride—and maybe even relax and enjoy it.*

SITUATION: After visiting colleges with your daughter, you have a hunch about one of them. You can see her enjoying and thriving at this school. The school offers everything she would want in a school: the right size, quality of education, and setting.

WISDOM: *Whenever possible, it is always a good idea to take a couple of days to carefully notice the intentions that motivate your comments, responses, and opinions to hunches and events.*

SITUATION: The college that you wanted to get into did not have the same feeling toward you. You got waitlisted.

WISDOM: *Whenever you experience great disappointment, you are attached to expectations of a specific outcome. If you don't build your world on expectations, it does not collapse when things turn out differently.*

SITUATION: After working very hard in high school, getting great grades, and participating in sports and activities, you do not get into your first choice for college. The bad news is devastating, and you feel hurt and ashamed. You wonder if all the hard work has been worth it.

WISDOM: *The great foolishness that people perpetuate is to make themselves unhappy because of their own reactions. Though a situation may not be in your control, your reaction to it is. Optional suffering comes from your reaction to situations; it is what you add on to whatever happens.*

SITUATION: A new college acquaintance will not be quiet about all her accomplishments from high school and how great her town and family are. She seems like a nice person, someone you could consider as a friend, but the constant bragging and inflated speech is getting tiresome.

WISDOM: *Have you known people whose ego was so overpowering that they could not stop speaking? Their ego is like a wild monkey that has gotten loose in the house of their mind. They need to put the monkey back in the jungle before it does any damage. Help them by treating them with loving kindness and compassion.*

SITUATION: On campus, a bulletin board advertises Spring Break activities. One ad is for a cruise in warm weather. Another is to help storm victims rebuild houses.

WISDOM: *With wisdom and awareness, you can see that there are skillful activities conducive to greater happiness and understanding—and there are unskillful ones that lead to suffering and conflict. Restraint is the capacity you have to discriminate one from the other, giving you the strength and composure of mind to pursue the skillful course.*

SITUATION: The clock will not go fast enough. It is Friday afternoon, and class just will not end so the weekend can begin.

WISDOM: *A major distraction in everyday life, and a hindrance to peaceful meditation, is restlessness—physical, mental, sometimes both. When you become aware of restlessness, you can short-circuit the stories in your mind and relax into your breath.*

SITUATION: In high school, you were extremely busy with sports, band, clubs, and schoolwork. But a lot of what you were involved in revolved around what was best for getting into college. Now that you are at college, you are excited that for the first time you can choose the extracurricular activities you want to get involved in.

WISDOM: *Avoid extremes so that you may realize a balance of mind and body, which brings peace and happiness. In all activity, practice calmness.*

SITUATION: During a college test, someone sitting next to you is obviously cheating off you. You know who this person is—a big sports figure on campus. You do not want to be a snitch, but it is not fair that you study so hard for your good grades and someone who probably did not even open the book will get a good grade on the test by cheating off you.

WISDOM: *A major obstacle to enlightenment is feeling cheated, holding a grudge. Maintain your integrity. Others live with their own karma.*

SITUATION: One of your roommates at college has taken a liking to her newfound freedom and is partying a little too much. Not only does her imbibing have a negative effect on her physically, it is also having a negative impact on her grades. She is going in a downward spiral. You and a group of friends, including the dorm resident assistant, decide to have an intervention with her before she hurts herself or gets kicked out of school.

WISDOM: *Pointing someone to their fundamental goodness will awaken it and help them find liberation and discover their true nature.*

SITUATION: Every time you go to the library to complete homework, you end up talking to your friends instead of doing the work. The conversations are fun, but your grades are beginning to suffer because you are not doing your homework at your best level.

WISDOM: *Why do you talk so much when you should be doing homework? When the inner and outer dialogues are going on, they hide loneliness, keep us from being bored or feeling afraid, and fill up all the space that is empty or scared. But they also block our hearts from opening and growing. You can only grow when things get quieter and you really see. Do your homework in silence with a relaxed mind and see how much more efficiently the task is completed.*

SITUATION: While studying in the library for final exams, you are distracted by a couple having a tiff a few tables from you.

WISDOM: *With distractions, remain an observer. Do not try to identify or name distractions. Do not react to a distraction or judge it. A distraction is just a distraction.*

SITUATION: It is getting late, and the paper that is due tomorrow is not yet done. You already gave up going out with your friends. Now it looks like you will be up most of the night working on your paper.

WISDOM: *Through the continued, willful exertion of effort, you sweat out your impurities and build a strong spirit, a willingness to overcome obstacles, a hunger to press on, a relentlessness on the path.*

SITUATION: You wanted to see an out-of-town concert just before final exams. Most of your friends didn't go because of finals, but you decided to go. You got back to school a day later than you anticipated because you carpooled with some other people and things happened that delayed your return. Now you are way behind in studying and writing your final paper. You have a feeling your grades are going to suffer big-time because of this adventure.

WISDOM: *Your problems are your own. You cannot ask anyone else to solve them for you or do the work for you. You have to do the work yourself.*

SITUATION: Your first year of college was so much fun that you can't believe it went by so fast. Socially, you are adapting well to the college environment. You feel that you are learning a tremendous amount academically, too, yet your grades are not reflecting this.

WISDOM: *Grades are important, but the real inspiration is in learning by doing. Become empowered to explore and experiment new ways of learning. Find teachers who not only teach but inspire.*

SITUATION: You do not know how you are going to make it through the semester. You have six classes plus a part-time job. The semester is a week old, and you already feel overwhelmed. You just want this semester to be over so that the pressure will be relieved.

WISDOM: *The journey is as important as the destination. The path becomes part of the goal. When you enjoy every moment, live life fully, and appreciate the journey, your mind will experience joyousness.*

SITUATION: College life is busy. Between studying, socializing, and sleeping, there is not much extra time. Nonetheless, you and your roommate are considering volunteering for the Big Brother/Big Sister program sponsored by your school.

WISDOM: *By doing a little good for others, you do a lot of good for yourself.*

SITUATION: You are having a terrible time at school. The work is hard, and on top of it, you get sick, putting you behind in your studies. Things are going from bad to worse, and you are becoming frustrated. When your parents call you, you don't want to talk. If they force you to have a conversation, you tend to take your frustrations out on them and make things worse.

WISDOM: *Get to the root of your frustration and stop the feelings. To start with, refrain from putting yourself first, and direct your frustration away from other people. Then go further and overcome your frustration.*

SITUATION: Your daughter wants to bring her car to college for the last two years. She is living off-campus and needs the car to commute to a part-time job and to school. You have said no to letting her take the car. You feel she does not really need it, and it is one more thing you do not want to worry about. But she is a good student and a responsible person.

WISDOM: *Be gentle, be kind, be thoughtful, be caring, be compassionate, be loving, be fair, be responsible, be generous—to everyone and yourself. Together you will work out the decision that makes the most sense in your particular situation.*

SITUATION: You are the first member of your family to go to college. Your parents came to the United States from a poor country that did not have many opportunities for people to pursue higher education. They worked hard so you could have opportunities that they did not have. You will be proud to graduate from college, a major accomplishment for both you and your parents.

WISDOM: *See your daily undertakings and long-range goals clearly and pursue them mindfully without making your happiness depend upon your expectations or those of others.*

SITUATION: You came from another country and moved to America in your teens. You remember what it was like to be in a foreign land and feel all alone. With the help of one particularly generous friend, you adapted quite well to your new home. At college, you have volunteered to show foreign exchange students around and make them feel at home.

WISDOM: *By demonstrating compassion and treating others as you would like to be treated, you can ease difficult experiences they may be encountering.*

SITUATION: It's the last semester of your senior year in college. You still have finals to go, and you just feel burnt out now.

WISDOM: *Tiredness is the product of a day filled with wasted thought, with feelings of anxiety and worry, anger and resentment. These negative mental states, whether openly expressed or inwardly held, do more to sap energy than anything else.*

SITUATION: After graduating from college, you feel lost. The only thing you really know how to do is to go to school, and now that is over. You do not have a job, and you have to move back home. It seems as if you have lost your path.

WISDOM: *Make a list of the things you have faith and trust in. Carry the list in your wallet or purse. When you are feeling spiritually lost, just pull it out and read it over until you feel better.*

SITUATION: You have just graduated from college. Your life has been pretty good up to this point. Now you want to develop a mission for the future.

WISDOM: *Sit and become silent. In a simple way, review the major areas of your current life—your schedule, work, finances, relationships, home, leisure activities, possessions, goals, and spirituality. For each, ask: "What would it be like to greatly simplify this area of my life?" Sit and reflect, just letting images or answers arise. After some time, then ask: "If it became simpler, would I be happy?"*

SITUATION: It seems like your life is in limbo. You just graduated from college, but you are not sure what kind of job you want or where you want to live. You are getting a little pressure from family and friends to get going with your life, but you just can't seem to take a step.

WISDOM: *Mindfulness can be used to find balance in your life. Mindfulness is being purposefully aware and noticing what you are experiencing and your response to those experiences. By living fully in each moment, you focus your effort on the present instead of insisting on what the future must be.*

SITUATION: You are considering going back to school for an advanced degree. It will help in your career path. You've already been away to college, and you do not feel that the college campus experience is important to you, so you are considering long-distance learning. Not only will an online college offer you more scheduling flexibility, it will also help lower your fuel cost because you will not be commuting to school.

WISDOM: *When you consume less of Earth's natural resources and lessen your carbon footprint, even a single day each week, you give the planet a much-needed respite from humankind's constant demands. When you protect Earth's environment, you begin to understand the intricate web of interrelatedness in the world.*

SITUATION: Winding down your graduate studies, burnout has crept in. You don't know how you are going to study for your oral exam because you are so weary of school.

WISDOM: *A natural light energy meditation is a good way to avoid burnout. Facing the sun on a bright day, breathe in its inexhaustible energy through all the pores of your body for 15 minutes. Feel the sun's energy convert into your energy. Feel your body become recharged by the sun's power.*

SITUATION: You have been taking pottery classes for a while, and you notice that you feel good before, during, and after class. You can't wait until you get to class.

WISDOM: *Those who are happy have their minds fixed on some object other than their own happiness: perhaps the happiness of others, the improvement of mankind, or even some art or pursuit followed not as a means but as an end in itself. By aiming at something else, they find happiness along the way.*

SITUATION: You knew being a new teacher was going to be a hard job. But winning over the students is proving more difficult than you imagined.

WISDOM: *Get into the habit of communicating in a meaningful and loving way. You will gradually develop inner qualities that give your words power, allowing them to influence and benefit others.*

SITUATION: You began college studying to become a teacher. Family members convinced you to switch majors and study business because, at the time, teaching did not pay well. Now you have a good business career, but you still regret not going into teaching.

WISDOM: *The livelihood you choose is an important opportunity to extend your spiritual practice. The choices you make about how you earn a living have a compelling potential for helping people. If you choose a livelihood that is ethical and does not harm others, you will be happy.*

SITUATION: As a student teacher, you are given a badly behaved class and no guidance from the administration. You make it through the eight weeks, but it is one of the worst experiences of your life. Not only do you not teach effectively, you also do not learn much from the experience. You are now questioning your career choice and judging yourself harshly.

WISDOM: *Do not judge yourself harshly. Judging yourself for being as you are is like judging the sky for its weather. Self-acceptance and spacious awareness allows you to experience your precious life as it is. Without mercy for yourself, you cannot love the world.*

SITUATION: One student in your class is the most disturbing child you have ever worked with. He negatively affects the entire class on an almost daily basis. You have tried everything to rectify the situation, to no avail.

WISDOM: *In an emotionally charged situation, focus your attention on the physical sensations in your body and on your own emotions, not on the situation or on those others involved. If you feel tension, bring your attention to that. Breathe and relax. Open yourself to find a creative solution or response to the challenge.*

SITUATION: You are trying to deal with a child who is very smart and has always gotten straight A's. Now your child is in high school, and he is still striving for perfect grades. Along with many other activities your child does, this quest for perfection is beginning to take its toll.

WISDOM: *Excellence is possible without perfection.*

SITUATION: At the school where you teach, there is a big fight between two groups of students during lunch. Things get pretty crazy, and emotions are running high. Students are extremely anxious for the rest of the day.

WISDOM: *When you touch base in any moment with the part of your mind that is calm and stable, your perspective changes immediately. You can see things more clearly and act from inner balance. Staying calm and stable while paying attention is key to resolving differences and misunderstandings.*

SITUATION: One of your students seems to get no encouragement from home to learn more or do better in school. As a teacher, it is discouraging and frustrating to watch this child struggle.

WISDOM: *When a friend supports and encourages another person in school, the desire to practice and learn more grows. Friendly support acts like the soil so the seed in the person can grow.*

SITUATION: As a teacher, you can usually tell when a parent helps too much with homework. You do not mind a little assistance from parents, because when a parent is there to answer questions or help out a little, it is a learning opportunity for the student. But when the help is too much, the student is hurt in the long run because the learning opportunity is missed. It is always tricky trying to relay this to parents who go beyond the limits of helpfulness.

WISDOM: *Avoid melodrama and generalization. Tell the parent honestly and compassionately what you think. Consider what sentences you would respond well to, and speak accordingly.*

SITUATION: As a high school English teacher, your favorite assignment is to have your students write their future obituaries and show how they want to be remembered. It is always satisfying to read about the good deeds these teenagers want to do in their lives. Over 95 percent of the students list great acts of charity or inventions to promote peace and eliminate hate and poverty. You hope that their goals will come true so the world becomes a better place for having them in it.

WISDOM: *We can all help create a wise and compassionate society by practicing inner peace, mindfulness, and respectfulness, leading to harmonious decisions that protect the most vulnerable members of society.*

Play

SITUATION: Even though you are frightened of water, someone convinced you to join them on a kayak outing.

WISDOM: *Have an ease and openness of mind that receives with interest every kind of circumstance. Ask what you can learn from each experience.*

SITUATION: After having been a competitive athlete your whole life, you are beginning to lose the passion for your sport. It is no longer fun when there is always a winner and loser.

WISDOM: *When passion fades, replace it with compassion.*

SITUATION: At your son's recent soccer game, you hear him say not-nice words to the goalie after the other team scores. Your son and the goalie are friends, but your son's words start a conflict between them. After the game, the two friends are not speaking to each other.

WISDOM: *When you begin to understand your role in a conflict, you will start to feel relief.*

SITUATION: The team you play for in college is a diverse crew. Currently, the team is not playing up to its potential because racial differences are having a negative impact.

WISDOM: *Relationships will fall apart if people are not respectful of each other's differences. With care and compassion, a warm heart and determination, difficult things can change, and healthy, happy people can talk through their differences, reaching a compromise that all can live with.*

SITUATION: Your daughter is a gifted athlete. She loves football, but the high school team only takes males. You feel that she would be able to compete with the boys if given the chance, so you are fighting the policy. It seems to be drawing a lot of attention, and your daughter is getting flack from every side, when the only thing she wants to do is play football.

WISDOM: *Awareness of the damage done by sexist remarks and attitudes helps bring us closer to not repeating them in the future.*

SITUATION: At school, you are being blamed by a teacher whom you like a lot for something you did not do. You know who the guilty person is, but you do not plan to tell the teacher. Not only are you angry at the teacher and the person who did the wrong act, but you feel bad because you are so angry at them.

WISDOM: *Experiencing angry thoughts does not make you an angry person as long as you let the angry thoughts pass through your mind.*

SITUATION: While your children are at the park playing, you sit down on a bench that is still wet with paint. A sign at the park's entrance said some of the benches were being painted, but the individual benches are not marked. You become angry at the people who painted the benches and take your children home immediately.

WISDOM: *Do not blame or get angry at others for your mistakes. All your problems are created by your own reactions. Absurdly, you blame the person who triggered the anger. It's impossible to get angry unless anger is waiting inside you to be triggered.*

SITUATION: After the softball game at the company picnic, members of the other team are laughing at you because your boss made a comment about you that you did not hear.

WISDOM: *We say someone "pushes our buttons," but your buttons only function because you believe some falsehood about yourself. When someone gets to you, they are pointing to a misconception you believe about yourself. Otherwise, they would have no power over you.*

SITUATION: During a performance in a local community play, your mind draws a blank and you forget your lines.

WISDOM: *Forgetting a line in a play does not mean that you have failed. It just means you forgot. Don't worry about it. Let it go and begin anew.*

SITUATION: Your father played soccer in high school and expects you to play, too. He has invested a lot of time coaching the teams you have played on throughout the years. You like soccer, but you don't love it anymore. You feel that you would be happier if you participated in a sport that did not consume all your time and energy so you could have time and energy to concentrate on your new love, music.

WISDOM: *Expectations that other have of you can be traps. Make the decision to be happy, and make your own happiness a factor in your decision making.*

SITUATION: You are a sports fanatic. The only programs you enjoy watching on television are sporting events. Your family does not share your enthusiasm for sports, though. They consider television sports to be obnoxious. Since you usually control the clicker, they do not have much say about what is watched on television.

WISDOM: *Under the wrong conditions, anyone is capable of acting like a jerk. Try to avoid the situations that turn you into a jerk. Respect and listen to your family.*

SITUATION: Since you were young, playing video games has been part of your leisure time. Now that you are an adult, you don't have as much time for them. Yet once you begin to play, time seems to stop, and hours can go by before you realize it.

WISDOM: *As with any addiction, the mind must become determined in its resolve to eliminate this negative behavior. Cease playing your video games, even temporarily, and use the time for mindful meditation. If you continue with meditation, the addiction will naturally fall away.*

SITUATION: Your son once loved basketball, but because a coach mistreated him and other team members, he has lost interest in the game. Your feelings of hatred toward this coach are strong because of what he did.

WISDOM: *If you cultivate hatred toward people, you start to live in a climate of hate. People will hate you in return. If you cultivate love toward people, you start to live in a climate of love. People will love you in return. It is your decision.*

SITUATION: Your coach is a yeller. Whatever you do is never good enough for him, so he yells at you. You don't really mind the yelling so much during practice because there are no spectators, but in a game when your parents and friends are there, it really bothers you.

WISDOM: *If you are having trouble with a coach, visualize the person and ask your subconscious for a color to describe that person. Once you see what energies are at work, as expressed by the color, you may be able to improve things.*

SITUATION: Near the end of your high school career, you are beginning to realize that you probably will not get that sports scholarship you were counting on to finance your college education. After all the time and energy you put into soccer, you are disappointed that your competitive playing days are probably numbered. You really thought that you had the talent to play big-time college soccer.

WISDOM: *Desire blinds you. Not getting what you deserve or desire can be disappointing. Happiness, then, is the confidence that pain and disappointment can be tolerated, that love will be the strength that gets you through.*

SITUATION: At baseball practice, your son is involved in an accident with a baseball bat, and his two front teeth are broken. Rushing him to the dentist's office, you cannot get the picture out of your head of what your son looks like with the broken teeth.

WISDOM: *The best discoveries are usually made by accident. A shocking situation brings out true compassion and love that you will never let go of.*

SITUATION: You are playing in a soccer game when, by accident, the ball bounces off you and goes into your own net, scoring a goal for the other team and losing the game for your team. Even though your coach and teammates try to console you, you feel terrible about what happened.

WISDOM: *Use gentleness and a sense of humor to settle down and stay present. Try to stay with the nakedness of your present-moment experience.*

SITUATION: Someone you know is downloading music onto your new iPod for you. You have a feeling that they are downloading illegally, but it is saving you a lot of money.

WISDOM: *Ethical conduct is a way of behaving that respects the right of others to happiness. Saving money is not as important as good karma.*

SITUATION: You are afraid of skiing—not the actual descent so much as going up the chairlift. For some reason, this fear is overwhelming to you. But everyone in your family loves skiing and goes often. When the rest of the family comes home after skiing, everyone is excited and has great stories to tell. You feel left out because of your fear.

WISDOM: *Try not to be the type of person who dies well before their physical death because fear consumes them.*

SITUATION: You love your purses. Since you were a little girl, having the right purse was always important to you. When you go to the movies, you feel more comfortable putting your purse on the seat next to you instead of on the floor. When the movie is crowded, you still try to make it look like someone is sitting in the seat next to you so you can keep your purse there.

WISDOM: *All suffering is caused by ignorance. People inflict pain on others in the selfish pursuit of their own happiness or satisfaction.*

Health

SITUATION: The flu threw you for a loop. It has been two weeks since you first got sick. You are no longer contagious, and most of the symptoms are gone, but you still feel like you were hit by a truck. It is as much mental as physical now.

WISDOM: *Take an active, positive role in healing your own mind, body, and spirit.*

SITUATION: You have been planning a dinner party for some weeks. Everything is set, but on the day of the party you get sick and have to cancel it.

WISDOM: *Realize that illness is inescapable, that stress around illness increases suffering, that being sick is not a shortcoming, and that you can be empowered by illness.*

SITUATION: Arthritis runs in your family. Now you are starting to feel the pain in your knees and fingers.

WISDOM: *Don't hate pain, fight it, or try to pretend it isn't there. Let it be, then let it go. Enter it, experience it, move through it.*

SITUATION: You bring your child to the doctor's office for his annual physical. According to the doctor, you have a physically healthy child. You feel so good and appreciative.

WISDOM: *Celebrate a diagnosis of good health from the doctor.*

SITUATION: You feel a lump on your breast during a self-examination. Terrified, you immediately make an appointment with a doctor.

WISDOM: *You cannot avoid illness, but you can reduce the fear it instills in you.*

SITUATION: Your aunt, who lives alone, has terminal cancer. Although it is extra work and an inconvenience, you still include her in many family activities.

WISDOM: *Help to alleviate your own suffering by helping to alleviate the suffering of others. Go and do something good for someone else.*

SITUATION: After being sick in bed for three days, the strength to get up is returning. You open the window blinds to look outside.

WISDOM: *Look out a window and see how wondrous life is. Be attentive to each moment, your mind clear as a calm river.*

SITUATION: One of your parents was just diagnosed with cancer. You realize that this can happen to anyone, especially aging parents, but it is still difficult to deal with.

WISDOM: *Not everything can be perfect. Bad things happen to everyone, and nobody likes them. How you handle those bad things is what causes your suffering, not the bad things themselves. Attaching to bad things, trying to control them, or letting them control you are the attitudes that cause suffering.*

SITUATION: Being in the medical field requires you to make split-second decisions that have life-and-death consequences for patients, and this takes a high emotional toll on you as a caregiver.

WISDOM: *The sense of well-being that comes with repeatedly bringing your mind to a state of calm and stillness begins to permeate everything else in your life.*

SITUATION: After a long marriage, just as you are about to retire, your spouse is diagnosed with Alzheimer's disease. You don't know how you are going to handle everything, especially on an emotional level.

WISDOM: *A healthy mind enables you to bear tragic events or bad news more easily, just as a strong body helps you resist sickness and recover more quickly. Whatever you cultivate during good times becomes your strength during bad times.*

SITUATION: Waiting to have a minor surgical procedure done, you are overcome by your fear of doctors, hospitals, and everything that can go wrong during an operation.

WISDOM: *Overcome fear by shifting your concern from yourself to others. When you see the difficulties that other people face, your own fears seem less important.*

SITUATION: Your busy life, including working and family responsibilities, does not leave much time for exercise. Over the years, the increase in weight and lack of exercise are beginning to take a physical as well as mental toll.

WISDOM: *The key to healthy living is learning how to change your state of mind.*

SITUATION: You need that late afternoon cup of coffee to get you through the rest of the day. But it is also affecting your sleep at night. You find yourself staying up way too late.

WISDOM: *If you know that your body is suffering because of the way you eat, sleep, or work, vow to eat, sleep, and work in healthier ways. Exercising, sleeping, and eating habits should be reasonable and conducive to physical health and social harmony.*

SITUATION: After suffering a major illness, your life and work goals have changed. What used to be important is no longer so important.

WISDOM: *If you bank on achieving genuine happiness and fulfillment by finding the perfect mate, getting a great car, having a big house, the best insurance, a fine reputation, the top job—if these are your focus, wish also for good luck in life's lottery.*

SITUATION: You have allowed your stress level to increase to the point where you are getting frequent headaches and stomachaches because of work and family pressure. The change is negatively affecting your overall health.

WISDOM: *Antidotes to suffering, stress, and anxiety include resisting less, grasping less, and identifying with things less.*

SITUATION: A friend of yours is trying to quit smoking. She has asked you to quit, too.

WISDOM: *Be patient with yourself while learning what drives your urges.*

SITUATION: You've reached a milestone: six straight months of vigorous exercise. Your body is beginning to change for the better. You've just finished a long bike ride and could use some comfort.

WISDOM: *Imagine taking a warm shower. As the water cascades over your body and down your legs, it carries with it all discomfort and distress, leaving you refreshed and invigorated.*

SITUATION: Summer is around the corner. After trying on your bathing suit to see if it fits, you decide a diet is a good and healthy thing to consider.

WISDOM: *Gradually shift to a diet of natural, healthy, simple, and appropriate food, away from highly processed foods, meat, and sugar, giving your body's chemistry time to adjust.*

SITUATION: High blood pressure runs in your family. You do not have high blood pressure now, but you do have a stressful job, and your diet is not as healthy as it could be. You decide that it is time to begin taking precautions.

WISDOM: *Practicing natural breathing in a comfortable position with your eyes closed and losing yourself so that you become untouched by day-to-day concerns is a way to deal with stress and high blood pressure.*

SITUATION: Getting enough sleep seems to be a challenge these days. Handling all the responsibilities and pressures that come with life is overwhelming. When you finally do get into bed, it is difficult to slow down your mind enough to get a good night's sleep.

WISDOM: *Sleep when you are tired, and listen to the rhythms of your body. Upon retiring, sleep as if you have entered your last sleep. Upon awakening, leave your bed behind you instantly as if you had cast away a pair of old shoes.*

SITUATION: This gives you cancer. No, wait—this does not give you cancer, but that does. No, wait, that may not give you cancer after all, but something else does. The media has your head spinning. You realize it's their job is to attract readers and viewers, but the conflicting information they give out is disturbing to you. One day they say one thing, the next day something else. After a while, you have no idea what to believe.

WISDOM: *Take nothing for granted. Question everything.*

SITUATION: After a cancer scare, you just don't feel like the same person you were before. You feel that it may be good to talk to a specialist about it.

WISDOM: *Sometimes an illness, whether minor or major, can change you. It can have either a positive or negative impact on your life. If you get lost during an illness, remind yourself that you are still the same person you were before.*

SITUATION: When you were younger, a diving accident in a pool left you paralyzed from the waist down. Now, in your late twenties, you are seeing your friends move on while you seem to be stuck. Some are getting married and starting families. Others are heading off on new adventures. You are happy for all your friends but sad for your own future.

WISDOM: *Your experience of life and emotions is shaped by how you perceive and how you think. If you want to transform your life, change how your mind perceives and thinks.*

SITUATION: Dementia runs in your family. Your father and an uncle were diagnosed with it. Presently, you show no symptoms of dementia, but you do want to take a proactive approach to improving your memory before any signs show up.

WISDOM: *There is scientific evidence that a regular meditation practice can ease the early symptoms of dementia and improve memory.*

SITUATION: You are about to have surgery that will make you no longer able to conceive a baby. You already have two healthy and beautiful children, and you need the surgery for health reasons, but it is still agonizing for you to deal with the fact that you will no longer be able to bear children.

WISDOM: *Take a few moments each day to think carefully about the good things you have: good relationships, special skills, good health, happy children. Be grateful for everything.*

SITUATION: Lately, you have been so anxious about work and personal problems that it is causing you physical problems. Even during downtime, you cannot relax. Your body is so tense that your muscles hurt. Even your jaw hurts from clenching it.

WISDOM: *An expert massage is a good way to relax. It enables your muscles to melt and your mind calm down. The accumulated stress in your body and mind will begin to leave as you guide yourself into healing. Relax like a great tree.*

SITUATION: Your parents have been smokers most of their adult lives. Now that you have a child of your own, you do not want her in their house when they are smoking. You figure this is the best time to help your parents quit the habit.

WISDOM: *Smoking endangers the health of smokers and those around them. Today, many people condemn smoking and view people who smoke unfavorably. You can encourage a person to quit smoking through a simple meditative technique. Whenever the desire to smoke arises, they should let the mind relax and enjoy that moment. After a while, the person may feel no need to smoke anymore.*

SITUATION: You began smoking because it was cool. Now it is just an unhealthy habit. When you smoke in public or outside your office, people look at you in a disgusted way, like you are doing something dirty. You don't like how you feel now when you smoke.

WISDOM: *Smoking is unhealthy for the person who smokes, as well as for family members, friends, and anyone else around who is exposed to secondhand smoke. It is also costly to society as a whole. The more you cultivate awareness of your mind and body in the present moment, the more you will become aware of the contradictions inherent in your smoking addiction. The reasons to stop smoking will become so obvious that you will realize you must quit.*

SITUATION: You are afraid to get actively involved in fighting AIDS because of the risk of contracting the HIV virus through some type of accident or mistake. You give monetary contributions for the fight but will not work with people who are infected with the disease.

WISDOM: *It is important to feel the joy of giving and charity. Not everyone is prepared to give to charities, and it should never be forced. When people are forced to give, they resent it and do not experience the joy of giving. It is okay to start small. Doing something is better than doing nothing. You will know when you are ready to give what you can.*

SITUATION: You feel angry when the dentist lectures you about your lack of flossing. You know that flossing helps keep your teeth and gums healthy, but you just don't like to stick your fingers in your mouth and floss. You are close to saying something harmful.

WISDOM: *Be as aware as possible of your thoughts and emotions so you can prevent harsh speech. When you are aware, you can notice the impulse to be cruel in your speech, especially when you are preoccupied.*

SITUATION: This is the most difficult decision you have ever had to make. Your husband of 50 years can no longer care for himself because of ill health. You are still relatively healthy, but you are becoming concerned about your own health—partly because of the effort, energy, and time it takes to care for your husband. Since he can no longer make decisions for himself, you decide that it is time for him to go into an assisted living environment. It is just breaking your heart, but deep down you know it is the best decision for all.

WISDOM: *Meet suffering compassionately, with an open heart. Genuine compassion acknowledges your emotions as well as your husband's. It offers you both comfort, where pity will do no such thing. If you give the gifts of love, compassion, and wisdom from your heart, your generosity will bear the fruit of happiness.*

SITUATION: It offends you to see billboards advertising medication for erectile dysfunction. You feel that these ads are inappropriate.

WISDOM: *Recognize your lack of control over the world. You can't stop the waves, but you can learn to surf.*

SITUATION: You cannot wait until you finally reach menopause. You are past the age that most women go through it, and a test indicates that you still have time before it begins. You are tired of going through the monthly cycles that you have endured all these years. You want to begin a new chapter in your life as a woman.

WISDOM: *By letting go of all you believe you are, by letting go of thinking you're the body or the mind, you become whole and you awaken. If you let go of everything, you can have anything. If you hold onto anything at all, you lose everything else, and that which you cling to changes and becomes a cause for pain.*

SITUATION: Your mother was recently diagnosed with early stage Alzheimer's. When people hear the diagnosis, they immediately assume that your mother is in full dementia. There is a major stigma attached to the disease, and your mother does not want people to treat her like she is stupid.

WISDOM: *An early diagnosis of a debilitating disease like Alzheimer's allows a patient to plan for her own future with dignity while she is still articulate enough to state what she wants. Those requests should be taken seriously and honored as her abilities diminish.*

SITUATION: Your father has had a debilitating physical illness for a number of years. The disease has progressed, leaving him in near bondage in his own body. The mind is still there, yet you have witnessed him go from a vibrant, active man to one for whom almost any physical movement takes monumental effort.

WISDOM: *It may be difficult to understand, but happiness does not depend on physical freedom. Happiness and inner freedom are not ultimately constrained by physical limitations. A disease can be a path to freedom, joy, and happiness.*

SITUATION: Since your father passed away, your mother has been taking medicine to help her deal with her depression because she feels so alone. You don't think the medicine is working very well. She was always a strong-willed person with a zest for life. What she is experiencing is more than sadness.

WISDOM: *With compassion, there is the potential of saving someone. She wants the inner pain and spiritual agony to stop. Relief comes in the form of leaving one's "self" and serving others. Can you find a way to get your mother to help others in this same situation?*

SITUATION: Your father is in terrible pain and suffering caused by incurable cancer. He is in hospice now, and the doctors say he does not have long to live. As you talk to your brother about your father's condition, the subject turns to assisted suicide. You wonder if you would consider assisted suicide if you were in your father's place.

WISDOM: *If there is no weighty karma, the mind states generated by wholesome or unwholesome actions in the last moments before death will condition rebirth. What karma comes with assisted suicide?*

SITUATION: Your grandmother and mother both had breast cancer, so you know it runs in the family. It just scares you to death, especially having young kids, that you may develop breast cancer and not be there for your children.

WISDOM: *When you experience or even think about unavoidable illnesses that are part of the human condition, be mindful of impermanence, free from fear, and grateful for the blessings that arise and pass away.*

ABOUT THE AUTHOR

Barbara Ann Kipfer, Ph.D. is a lexicographer, archaeologist, and practicing Buddhist. She has written more than 25 books, including *1325 Buddhist Ways to Be Happy* and *201 Little Buddhist Reminders*. She lives in New York City.